Long Live The National

Also by John Hughes
MY GREATEST RACE

Also by John Hughes and Peter Watson
MY GREATEST TRAINING TRIUMPH

Long Live The National

John Hughes and Peter Watson

with a Foreword by
HRH The Prince of Wales

Michael Joseph ▪ London

First published in Great Britain by
Michael Joseph Limited
44 Bedford Square,
London W.C.1
1983

ISBN 0 7181 2231 3

Filmset and printed by BAS Printers Ltd, Hampshire
Bound by Hunter and Foulis Ltd, Edinburgh

Contents

List of Colour Illustrations

Photographic Acknowledgements

The authors would like to thank all those who supplied photographs from their private collections; in addition, they would like to thank the following for other photographs in this book. The folios refer to the pages on which they appear:

Fox Photos: 14–15, 24 (top), 30 (top), 31, 52, 54–5, 72 (left), 74 (bottom), 75, 83, 104, 115, 133, 175, 186, 187; *The Times*, 20, 56; Central Press, 21, 22–3, 24 (bottom), 25, 26, 27, 82, 90, 109, 154 (top), 174, 181; Keystone: 28, 29, 30 (bottom), 60, 68, 73, 78, 89, 103, 130, 137 (bottom), 141, 142, 179, 180; George Selwyn, 36, 100 (top), 196; Sporting Pictures: 33, 35, 38, 48, 62, 66 (bottom), 67, 117, 136, 170, 198; *Daily Express*: 42, 44, 45, 63, 87, 98, 122, 128, 129, 132, 140, 159, 176 (bottom), 199, 201; Bernard Parkin: 47, 66 (top), 126; Associated Newspapers: 51, 106–7, 116, 151; S & G Press Agency: 57, 74 (top), 84, 88, 92, 110, 118, 149, 153, 154 (bottom), 176 (top), 182, 192; BBC Hulton Picture Library: 58; *Sun*: 61; Press Association: 72 (right), 162; Kemsley Newspapers: 79; Ladbrokes: 9, 32, 94, 95, 112, 165; *Liverpool Post*: 100 (bottom), 102; Topical: 107, 146; Alec Russell: 124; Primrose Productions Ltd: 150; W. Everitt: 169, 188 (left & right), 189, 197.

Acknowledgements

We are honoured that HRH The Prince of Wales so readily agreed to write the Foreword to this book; his admiration for the sport is well-known. Our warmest thanks go to all those who agreed to share their greatest Grand National memories, enabling us to re-live many of the most fascinating Aintree tales of recent years and to present them, for the first time, in one collection.

We would like to thank the *Sunday People* for permission to quote from Jonathan Powell's interview with Bob Champion, and Jonathan and Bob themselves and Victor Gollancz Ltd for permission to quote from *Champion's Story*; and the *Sunday Telegraph* for permission to reproduce the article by John Oaksey.

Finally, but by no means least, our admiration is unbounded for those courageous horses without which there would be no memories at all.

John Hughes & Peter Watson

Foreword by
H R H The Prince of Wales

I must confess to feeling rather awkward in writing a foreword to this splendid book. I cannot escape from the fact that whatever I say has probably been said far better already – and by people far better qualified, who have actually taken part in this extraordinary steeplechase. I can only speak from the point of view of an enthusiastic spectator and as one who has the greatest possible admiration for the horses and jockeys who participate. It is only in the last five or six years that I have come to appreciate the real significance of the Grand National and of its deep roots in the sporting life of Britain. It is, indeed, a typically British 'institution'. In other words, it developed almost by accident and in a very small way at the beginning. Gradually it grew in the affections of the public – and the bookmakers! – to the extent that it would be impossible to sit down and invent a race like it if you wanted to start from scratch.

That is what makes the whole thing unique, together with the fact that the race has continued to be run over fences that were originally part of the natural countryside, thereby providing the character and challenge which makes it a race that so many people find irresistible. No other steeplechase produces the emotional and electric atmosphere that surrounds Aintree and no other race produces such a vast betting interest.

There is much talk at present about the fearsome problems which surround the Grand National – but then it always seems to have been surrounded by endless complications. The point is that we simply must not let these problems destroy something which is a glorious, and somewhat eccentric, part of our heritage. I hardly dare say that we would all be the poorer for it because I can think of many thousands of punters who would probably be considerably less impoverished! Nevertheless, we would lose something which is irreplaceable anywhere else; the whole racing fraternity would lose their greatest adrenalin-producing challenge; many people's dreams and ambitions would be forever frustrated (after all, my great great grandfather, when Prince of Wales, won the Grand National in 1900 with Ambush II . . .!) and we would be denied the indescribable, tingling thrill of seeing those gallant horses fly over a series of astonishing obstacles.

This book captures the flavour of an occasion which has fired the imagination of successive generations and given rise to countless stories of legendary exploits, all of which form a rich pattern in our national consciousness. Long may it all continue for the inspiration of our successors!

Charles.

THE GRAND NATIONAL
by Peter Watson

There have been enough sentimental tears to float Aintree into the River Mersey; enough cheers to deafen the sounds of Concorde. For the best part of two centuries, the Grand National has heaved and tugged at our emotions, the supreme test for one man and his horse.

It never fails to thrill us; it's often cruel to be kind. It rarely fails to surprise us, its demands cannot be matched anywhere in the world.

Aintree spreads like some neglected prairie across 270 acres of the outskirts of industrial Liverpool; almost silent, friendless for 364 days of the year. National Day and it comes alive in a blaze of colour; people pour over the pear-shaped course from all parts of the world, jostling for a sight of those taking part in the greatest steeplechase in the world where thirty fences, spread menacingly over the heartbreaking four-and-a-half miles, stand between rider and horse and a place in racing folklore.

It is an incredible story which goes back to 1829 when William Lynn, the proprietor of the Waterloo Hotel near Aintree, leased land from the second Earl of Sefton and began to organise race meetings on the flat. Lynn introduced steeplechasing to his programme in 1836 and the following year staged the race which some historians cite as the first National.

Lynn persuaded the civic authorities of Liverpool to support the race and Viscount Molyneux, eldest son of the Earl of Sefton, acted as umpire. Lynn drew up the following conditions: 'A Sweepstake of 10 sovs each with £100 added by the Town of Liverpool for horses of all denominations, 4 years old, 11st; 5, 11st 7lb; 6 and aged 12st., Gentlemen Riders. Over a country not exceeding five miles, to be chosen by the umpire or such other persons as he may appoint. The ground to be shown to the riders on the morning of the race, and the umpire to have the power of ordering them to start.'

The first Great Liverpool Chase in 1837 was won by The Duke at a distance estimated at '30 yards' with Cheshire amateur Henry Potts on board. Sir William and his owner-rider from Galway, Alan McDonough, is credited with victory in 1838 but since both races were run at Maghull some miles from Aintree, the

Topham family who are synonomous with the National, insist on 1839 as the authentic running of the first National.

Lynn resigned from management of the 1839 race and the race committee was headed by the local notables – the Earls of Derby and Sefton, Lord George Bentinck and Lord Robert Grosvenor. There were seventeen starters from an original entry list of fifty-five, and they set out over a course of twenty-nine jumps which included three brooks and a 5-ft stone wall which was jumped only on the first circuit. The added money for the race was the same in 1837 although it cost more to enter – a sweepstake of twenty sovereigns each.

The course has changed little over the years although it is interesting to recall the words of Finch Mason – who was to own two National winners, Peter Simple (1849) and Miss Mowbray (1852) – in 1845: 'Since the preceding year, sundry alterations have been made. There was then one field of turf on leaving the course, and one previous to entering it. In the first of these, the turf had been pared off by the plough, in the second by the spade and the square lumps of turf and soil being loosely scattered about, made it as uneven and distressing a piece of ground for horses to gallop over as is possible to conceive. Every other field in the line was fallow, with the exception of the two previous to Becher's Brook which were of wheat. Several of the rails on the bank were removed, and the line was on the whole a decidedly easy one.' Mason's reference to different fields demonstrates how the original steeplechase courses comprised natural country with semi-artificial fences which were only altered slightly from their natural shape. Steeplechases were for hunters and run over 'fair hunting country'.

The origin of Aintree's famous drop fences evolved in the natural difference in levels of the land where the field on the landing side or drop side was lower than that on the take-off. There was no inside rail or running rail in the early years and the fences which were higher in some parts than others were marked only by a flag which the riders had to go outside. The first major alterations to the fences took place in time for the 1864 Grand National when the course contained seven hurdles as part of the total of thirty fences.

It was almost one hundred years and a thousand thrills later before the next severe alterations to the fences – in 1961. They were then sloped away on the take-off side, having originally been almost perpendicular, to give horses an extra two feet or so in which to gain enough height in the air to clear them. Previously, if a horse got too close to a fence, it stood no chance of negotiating it safely.

The modern National course contains sixteen fences on the first circuit of which the first fourteen are jumped again second time round, the two circuits providing a journey of four miles and 856 yards. There is a run of 471 yards from the starting gate to the first fence when hope springs eternal, and a haul of 494 yards from the last fence to the winning post when fulfilment seems an eternity away.

The first few races were either weight for age contests or all horses carried 12st with the exception of brave Lottery who was required to carry an 18lb-penalty in 1841 and 1842 for winning the Cheltenham Steeplechase; the race became a handicap in 1843, however, and has remained so ever since though in 1857, for example, the top weight was 11st 2lb and the bottom weight 8st 10lb. For years, the top weight was 12st 7lb but from 1961 that was reduced to 12st with a bottom weight of 10st.

The race was called The Liverpool and National Steeplechase for the first time in 1843 and four years later was finally named the Grand National Handicap Steeplechase. Enthusiasm grew and in 1874 a group of twenty-four National Hunt committee members wrote to Messrs. Topham – the family first became associated with the management side of the race in 1856 though Edward William Topham was in fact a member of the syndicate which staged the 1839 race – complaining of the danger caused by spectators crowding fences due to the lack of railings. It was 1885 before the whole course was railed in.

The course fell into disrepute during the 1850s and early 60s but the formation of the National Hunt Committee in 1866, with an official Calendar and code of Rules, revived the sport and Aintree was thriving by the 1890s. War closed the course after the 1915 National and three substitute races were run at Gatwick on the site of the modern airport but the course bore no resemblance to Aintree; it was right-handed with a short run-in and no hazards to compare with the Canal Turn or the drops down to the landing side at Becher's and Valentine's. Prize money at Gatwick for the Racecourse Association Steeplechase was limited to £500 compared with the £3500 then associated with the National proper.

The twenties and thirties were halcyon days for the National which was run on a Friday before vast crowds. War again interrupted the National between 1941 and 1945 and the fortunes of the World's Greatest Steeplechase began to decline. The Topham family had managed the course for almost a century when, in 1949, the seventh Earl of Sefton sold them – for under £300,000 – the land which had belonged to his family since racing began at Aintree. The sale was subject to a covenant restricting its use to racing and agriculture and, sadly, the great race has more often than not been clouded in uncertainty ever since.

The attraction of armchair viewing – the National was first televised in 1960, the first radio broadcast having gone out in 1927 – had a marked effect on attendances and Mirabel Topham, the racecourse manager since 1951, stunned the world of racing by announcing her intention to sell Aintree for development

Becher's, the most famous National fence of all: Anthony Mildmay and Davy Jones lead the 1936 field round the unfenced course

in 1964, insisting that it was hopelessly uneconomic to maintain Aintree as a racecourse.

Lord Sefton immediately contested the planned sale in the law courts; he sought an injunction to restrain Mrs Topham and was given judgement which was upheld in the House of Lords but reversed on appeal in 1966. Lord Sefton's covenant was ruled not binding in law. The legal battle thus caused a delay and the 1965 race became the first in a long, sad line of 'last' Grand Nationals. Mrs Topham battled on to make Aintree profitable but received little help. Admission prices rose and television coverage became so excellent that the public stayed away, and in November 1973 Mrs Topham finally cried 'enough' and sold the course to Bill Davies's Walton Group for around £3 million.

Mr Davies ran the race for two years but another massive increase in admission prices kept racegoers away and, late in 1975, Mr Davies announced that his company would not be prepared to lose more money by underwriting the race in 1976. The end seemed nigh; deadlines came and went as the racing industry first called Mr Davies's bluff and then set about the unthinkable, laying plans for a substitute race on another course with Doncaster, Newcastle and Haydock Park named the likely alternatives. A committee had already been appointed to make the choice when on 22 December 1975 the bookmakers, Ladbrokes, announced a deal with Mr Davies – they would pay an annual six-figure fee for the right to manage the Grand National for seven years.

John Hughes, who was already running Lingfield Park for Ladbrokes, was installed as Clerk of the Course and, working at breakneck speed, he attracted a host of sponsors and a meeting worthy of the National. By 1977, Hughes had put together a festival of jumping to complement Cheltenham and the crowds once again flocked to Aintree.

But, by the winter of 1981, the future of the National was once more called into question. Ladbrokes announced that they would not renew their management contract – and Mr Davies put an £8 million price tag on the course, several millions more than racing's Levy Board were prepared to pay to take on the home of the world's greatest steeplechase. Then on 24 March 1982, the Jockey Club revealed they had reached agreement with Mr Davies for an option to buy Aintree – and would endeavour to raise the money by a world-wide appeal. They signed with Mr Davies on the morning of the National, but the haggling continued throughout the summer. The 1983 race was only given the go-ahead on Friday 5 November 1982 when the parties agreed on a £4 million deal. This sum would need to be raised through public subscription by 1 May 1983.

A few hours after the agreement had been signed, thirty-nine horses lined up; once more there were tears and cheers as Grittar and amateur rider Dick Saunders battled up the run-in to a place in history, the latest in a long line of horses and men which began with Lottery and Jem Mason winning easily in 1839 . . .

Previous page: The stands were packed to overflowing as thirty horses and riders set out for the 1940 race

What a day that must have been – Tuesday 26 February 1839. Roads to Aintree were jammed and an estimated 50,000 people crowded on to the racecourse. One newspaper story of the time reported guests sleeping 'four to a bed' in local hostelries. The race, due off at one o'clock, was more than two hours late starting.

Captain Becher, one of the leading riders in the early days of organised chasing, dashed off into the lead on his horse Conrad with one of the Irish challengers, Daxon. Both horses took off at the first brook together – but Conrad dumped Captain Becher in the brook on the landing side and it has been Becher's Brook ever since! Becher remounted Conrad and almost caught Lottery even then, before parting company with his horse once more, leaving Lottery to stroll away to win from Seventy-four and the legendary Black Tom Olliver, who was to ride in nineteen Grand Nationals, winning three of them – in 1842, 1843 and 1853.

Olliver's mount in 1853 was Peter Simple who was winning the race a second time, just as Abd el Kader had done with victories in 1850 and 1851. Olliver passed on his Aintree know-how to George Stevens who rode in the race fifteen times and registered a record five victories. Stevens began the sequence on Free Trader in 1856 and won in successive years, 1863 and 1864, on the full sisters Emblem and Emblematic. Then Stevens became the first man to win in consecutive years on the same horse – The Colonel in 1869 and 1870.

There was no one quite like Tom Scott, a popular local sportsman, who performed a quite extraordinary feat in 1870 by jumping, horseless, one circuit of the National for a bet . . . there is no record of the time he took!

The 1871 National featured the 'dream horse', The Lamb, who had already won three years earlier but missed both the 1869 and 1870 races. Two years after The Lamb's 1868 victory, his rider, Mr George Ede who rode as Mr Edwards, was killed during Aintree's Sefton Chase. So the owner, Lord Poulett, had to find another rider for the 1871 National.

It is recorded that three months before the race his Lordship had two dreams. In the first, The Lamb finished last but in the second he finished first by four lengths and Lord Poulett reported that he saw not only his colours of cerise and blue but also the jockey wearing them – Mr Tommy Pickernell, who rode as Mr Thomas. He wrote to Mr Pickernell the following day, telling of his dreams and asking him to ride the horse at Aintree. Pickernell agreed. And on the day of the race, a crowd of racegoers arriving at one of the Liverpool stations saw a lamb escape from a truck in a siding and race around the railway lines; The Lamb started second favourite and won easily!

The name of the Beasley family was to be etched in the history of the National for the first time in 1879 when the brothers Tommy, Harry, Willie and Johnny Beasley each rode in the race that year. Collectively the brothers rode four winners, six seconds and two thirds between 1877 and 1892 from a total of thirty-four rides – and sixty-nine years later, Harry's grandson, Bobby, won on Nicolaus Silver, the first grey to win for ninety years. It is perhaps not without significance for an event which transcends the very essence of sportsmanship that there has been but one objection to the result of the National – when Captain Roddy Owen on Cloister lodged one to Come Away and Harry Beasley in 1891. It was disallowed.

The magnificent Cloister, second again in 1892, returned to win in 1893, making virtually every yard of the running and becoming the first horse to win under 12st 7lb. His winning time of 9 minutes 32.4 seconds was the fastest since the distance was altered in 1863 and his margin of victory a record forty lengths. After Cloister there was Manifesto, who was fourth on his first tilt at the race in 1895. He suffered his first and only Aintree fall a year later but won the following year and again in 1899, having missed the 1898 National through injury. Like Cloister, Manifesto carried 12st 7lb in 1899.

The Prince of Wales, meanwhile, who would become King Edward VII in 1901, had been keen to win steeplechasing's premier prize ever since his first visit to Aintree in 1878. And 1900 was his year. Manifesto, then a twelve-year-old, made a gallant attempt to win under 12st 13lb while the Prince's horse, Ambush II, seventh behind Manifesto in 1899, received 20lb. Manifesto and Ambush II were locked together as they jumped the last but that long run-in beat Manifesto just as it had denied so many before and since, and Ambush II drew clear on the flat. The heroic Manifesto was eased twenty yards from the line and passed for second place by the lightweight Barsac. Manifesto graced Aintree until 1904 when he finished unplaced behind the New Zealand-bred Moifaa; he had run in eight Grand Nationals, winning two, finishing third three times and fourth once.

The National has never fallen to the weather though it was postponed several times during the early days. There were those who felt the 1901 race should not have been run though Mr J. B. Bletsoe, the owner and breeder of the successful horse, Grudon, would not be among them. The race was run in a snowstorm and the course thick under a blanket of white. Mr Bletsoe packed his horse's hooves with butter to prevent the snow packing like ice within the shoe and Grudon raced home like a cat through rain to give jockey Arthur Nightingall his third National.

An American-bred horse won the National for the first time when Rubio triumphed in 1908. Yet Rubio, bred in California, was originally knocked down to Major Frank Douglas-Pennant, the future Lord Penrhyn, for fifteen guineas as a potential hunter; after hunting as a four-year-old, he was sent to a Leicester repository for sale with a reserve of sixty guineas. There was no offer so Rubio was put in training and promptly broke down. He was then loaned to the landlord of the Towcester hotel to run in harness.

Three years later and many miles of road work having helped him to return to fitness, Rubio was back in training with Fred Withington near the old Stockbridge racecourse in Hampshire. He was entered for the National with stable companion Mattie Macgregor. Stable jockey L. W. N. Bissill was given the choice of mounts – and picked Mattie Macgregor, who finished second, while Bernard Bletsoe, son of the owner of Grudon, rode Rubio.

The following year was the turn of the French and Lutteur III, a five-year-old. Mr J. Hennessy sent the horse over from his French trainer George Batchelor well before Aintree and Lutteur III won his preliminary race at Hurst Park before completing his Aintree preparation with the trainer Harry Escott at Lewes.

Two years later in 1911, there is another landmark in the story of the Great Race – for the first time, only one horse completed the course without mishap. The survivor and victor was Frank Bibby's Glenside, the stable second string, ridden at the last moment by a young Welshman Jack Anthony in place of Tich Mason, who broke a leg shortly before the race. Rathnally, Shady Girl and Foolhardy had to be remounted to finish second, third and fourth – and those four were the only finishers. Anthony rode his second National winner in 1915 on Ally Sloper in the colours of Lady Nelson, widow of Sir William Nelson, making her the first woman owner to win the race which then fell victim to the war and the War Office assumed temporary occupation of Aintree.

Three substitute races at Gatwick owe only a sentimental place in the National Story though the third winner there, Poethlyn, went to Aintree when the race returned home in 1919 and won comfortably with Ernie Piggott – Lester's grandfather – in the saddle. It was Piggott's second National for he had won on Jerry M in 1912, both Poethlyn and Jerry M carrying 12st 7lb. Then Jack Anthony completed his hat-trick on Troytown in 1920.

The National entered its finest hour for the twenties and thirties were an age of huge fields, great horses and the growth of American interest. The National was run on a Friday before enormous crowds.

Sergeant Murphy in 1923 became the first American-owned horse to win the National – he was the property of former Cambridge University undergraduate Stephen Sandford – and his rider, the leading amateur, Captain G. H. 'Tuppy' Bennet, steered a middle course at Aintree with unflinching courage. Captain Bennet, alas, had a fall in a four-horse race at Wolverhampton on Boxing Day the same year, was kicked in the head by a following horse and died a fortnight later with a smashed skull. That incident, following other serious head injuries to steeplechase jockeys, forced the National Hunt Committee to make skull caps compulsory equipment.

The American connection was maintained in 1926 when Jack Horner – bought for 4000 guineas by Newmarket trainer Jack Leader on behalf of American Charlie Schwartz – improved on his seventh placing in 1925 to win from Old Tay Bridge. But Leader never saw the finish . . . an overjoyed Schwartz slapped

1929, and the biggest field in the history of the National. The sixty-six runners had to line up in two rows

him so hard on the back that Leader fell off his place in the stand!

The legendary Tipperary Tim, a 100–1 shot, came home alone in 1928 after the brilliant Easter Hero, who was to win the Gold Cup in 1929 and 1930, became stuck on top of the Canal Turn fence, putting most of the field out of the race. Billy Barton, a last fence faller, was remounted to finish second. The ditch on the take-off side of the Canal Turn was filled in the following year when Gregalach won from a record field of sixty-six with the very same Easter Hero second, despite spreading a plate half a mile from home. The crowd was estimated at a staggering 300,000.

The minimium weight was increased to 10st 7lb in 1931 and, a year later, entry was restricted to horses which had been placed in a 3 mile Chase worth £200 or more, or in a Chase of any distance at Liverpool.

The name of Rimell, later destined to go hand-in-hand with the National, appeared on the honours board for the first time in 1932 when Tom Rimell sent Forbra up from Kinnersley to beat Egremont after a stirring battle.

1929 and every one of the 66 starters safely negotiated the first fence

Kellsboro' Jack (1933), Reynoldstown (1935 and 1936), Royal Mail (1937) and Battleship (1938) – the latter being the first horse both owned and bred in the United States to triumph – all graced the National in the thirties but the era was dominated by Golden Miller, the winner of the Gold Cup in five consecutive years between 1932 and 1936.

Golden Miller made his first appearance at Aintree under top weight of 12st 2lb in 1933 – and came down for the first time in his life at the Canal Turn on the second circuit. Golden Miller's owner, Dorothy Paget, sent him back to Aintree the following year; he again had 12st 2lb and once more the punters made him favourite. And this time they were right, Gerry Wilson steering Golden Miller home in a record 9 minutes 20.4 seconds – the first and only horse to win the Gold Cup and Grand National in the same year – surely meriting his title as Horse of the Century.

Golden Miller returned in 1935, was asked to shoulder 12st 7lb, and unseated Wilson at the eleventh. Wounded punters who had made him 2–1 favourite

voiced the view that the great horse was not suited to Aintree so the redoubtable Miss Paget saddled him again the following day for the Championship Chase . . . and Golden Miller unseated Wilson at the first fence! It took Golden Miller two more years to emphatically prove his aversion to Aintree – he fell at the first in 1936, was remounted and then refused at the eleventh, and fell again at the bogey eleventh in 1937.

Reynoldstown's place in National folklore is secure as one of only seven horses to win the Aintree marathon more than once though his victory in 1936 surely had the touch of luck even though his jockey thought he would have won anyway. That jockey was Fulke Walwyn, then a subaltern in the 9th Lancers and one of the greatest National Hunt trainers of our time who sent out Team Spirit to win the 1964 National. Frank Furlong, who had ridden Reynoldstown to his first triumph – the horse was owned and trained by his father, Major Noel Furlong – had trouble with his weight and quit riding. Most people at Aintree thought that Walwyn seemed booked for second place as Reynoldstown and the 100–1 outsider Davy Jones headed for the second last fence. Davy Jones had been bought for £650 by Lord Mildmay of Flete for his son Anthony Mildmay to ride and try to achieve a lifelong ambition by winning the National; Davy Jones pecked at the second last, the buckle of the reins snapped and the rudderless Davy Jones, ran out at the last fence leaving Walwyn and Reynoldstown to collect.

Queen Elizabeth the Queen Mother has, down the years, been the most marvellous supporter of National Hunt racing, and with King George VI saw Royal Mail's victory in 1937. A year later, seventeen-year-old Bruce Hobbs became the youngest rider ever to win the National when he steered Battleship home from the Irish-trained Royal Danieli, ridden by Dan Moore, who was himself destined to become a successful trainer at the Curragh, saddling L'Escargot to win the National in 1975.

The 1939 National was run amid fears of a second World War and was won by Workman who had once been sold for £26. The fears were realised later that year and steeplechasing was, at first, allowed to continue and Bogskar won in 1940 for Lord Stalbridge, the first peer to own and train a National winner. It was the last National for six years.

Aintree crowds were back to twenties' and thirties' proportions in the immediate post-war period but then the fortune of the world's greatest steeplechase began to decline. Historically, the National had always been the most valuable and prestigious race in the steeplechasing calendar, inevitably attracting the best horses. But the successful development of the Cheltenham

The Twenties and Thirties were halcyon days for the National, which was run on a Friday before vast crowds, and 1925 was no exception. The stands are packed, almost entirely by men

Top left: Royal Mail over Becher's second time round on the way to victory in 1937

Bottom left: Golden Miller winning in 1934, the only horse ever to win the National and the Cheltenham Gold Cup in the same year

Below: H.M. Queen Elizabeth the Queen Mother in the paddock with H.M. The Queen before the 1955 race. Her horse, M'as-tu-vu, stands quietly

Gold Cup, along with the advent of sponsored races, particularly in the south, provided enticing counter-attractions for owners and trainers who were reluctant to risk their best horses around Aintree's feared circuit.

The gloom was yet to come, however, as Prince Regent attempted to emulate Golden Miller in 1946 by adding the National to his Cheltenham Gold Cup triumph. Prince Regent, who was rated at the time by his trainer Tom Dreaper as the best he had trained, had 12st 5lb and was giving 21lb or more to all but two of his rivals in a field of thirty-four horses. The eleven-year-old ran a magnificent race; he was so far ahead passing the Anchor Bridge turn that he looked sure to win. He took the last, four lengths ahead of Lovely Cottage but that cruel run-in claimed another victim and Lovely Cottage caught and passed Prince Regent, who was even denied second place by Jack Finlay. Prince Regent carried 12st 7lb into fourth place behind the 100–1 winner Caughoo in 1947 when, at the request of the Labour Government, the National was moved from Friday to Saturday. The following year, Prince Regent ran out.

Sheila's Cottage, the first mare to win the National since Shannon Lass in 1902,

Sheila's Cottage and a smiling Arthur Thompson are led in after winning in 1948, the first of trainer Neville Crump's three National victories

put Neville Crump on the National map in 1948, Teal (1952) and Merryman II (1960) completing a notable hat-trick. But even Captain Crump's achievement was surpassed – by the brilliant Vincent O'Brien, who sent out Early Mist, Royal Tan and Quare Times to win in successive years from 1953.

The Grand National has played its tricks in a multitude of ways but none more bizarre than Devon Loch's demise in 1956. The Queen Mother's magnificent animal had the race won, the cheers rang out, hats were raised, when, inexplicably, Devon Lock sank to the ground fifty yards from the winning line. We will never know what really happened; the record books coldly proclaim that ESB ran on to give Fred Rimell the first of his record-breaking four victories – Aubrey Hastings' four winners include Ballymacad at Gatwick in 1917 – and jockey Dave Dick became the only man in history to ride a Grand National and a Lincoln winner. The Russians sent two horses – Reljef and Grifel – in 1961 but neither completed the course as Nicolaus Silver became the first grey to win since The Lamb in 1871 to give Rimell victory No. 2.

Fred Winter's love affair with the National began in 1957 when he rode

H.M. Queen Elizabeth the Queen Mother with her jockey, Dick Francis, before the 1956 race. Left to right: Bill Braddon, Squadron Leader Christopher Blount, Lord Abergavenny talking to Peter Cazalet, H.M. Queen Elizabeth the Queen Mother, Princess Margaret, Dick Francis, H.M. Queen Elizabeth talking to Arthur Freeman (hidden), Lord Sefton

Sundew to victory, the horse having fallen on his two previous appearances in the race. Winter was in the winner's enclosure again in 1962 on Kilmore following a race in which age and experience counted for an awful lot after a journey through the mud. Kilmore, a twelve-year-old, won from the twelve-year-old Wyndburgh with another twelve-year-old, Mr What, in third place.

Maybe steeplechasers are like good wine; Fred Winter certainly is, for he no sooner started training than he was winning the National in successive years – first with Jay Trump in 1965 and then with Anglo. A magnificent achievement.

The 1967 National is etched forever in the memory of Aintree folklore for the horrendous pile-up at the twenty-third – the fence after Becher's second time round. Two loose horses ran down the fence and all those following but one, the 100–1 outsider Foinavon who paid 444–1 on the Tote and had been almost tailed off at the time, was impeded. There were horses and jockeys everywhere but John Buckingham threaded Foinavon through the moving horror, up and over the fence, and away for an unbelievable victory. Foinavon, poor chap, was generally regarded the most moderate National winner of all – neither his owner, Cyril

Red Rum, the king of Aintree, returns to the stables at the back of Ginger McCain's car showrooms in Southport after a work-out on the sands

Watkins nor his trainer, John Kempton had bothered to go to Aintree, the trainer's father saddling the horse. Foinavon was only the second blinkered runner to win the race, Battleship (1938) being the other.

Brian Fletcher, then nineteen, arrived on the Aintree scene in 1967 finishing third on Red Alligator before winning on the same horse the following year. The same Brian Fletcher drove Red Rum past the gallant Crisp in the last strides to win in 1973 in a record 9 minutes 1.9 seconds – a speed of nearly 29 miles an hour over the thirty toughest obstacles in the world; the record still stands.

The most romantic chapter in the National Story had begun. True, Gay Trip (1970) and Rag Trade (1976) were to complete Fred Rimell's four-timer; Well To Do (1972) and Ben Nevis (1980) were to give Tim Forster a training double; Aldaniti and Bob Champion – awarded the MBE in 1982 – were to write their own fairy-tale in 1981; Dick Saunders was to become, at forty-eight, the oldest winning

1976 and the final fence in the world's greatest steeplechase: Rag Trade and John Burke, left, and Red Rum, ridden by Tommy Stack, take it together before Rag Trade ran on to give trainer Fred Rimell his fourth Aintree triumph

rider in the history of the race in 1982. But Red Rum was something else. He won again in 1974, was second to L'Escargot and Rag Trade the following two years and then carried 11st 8lb to an historic third victory in 1977 – the only horse to win the Great Race three times.

The racing world fell in love with Rummy from the moment he came out of Ginger McCain's extraordinary little stable behind a car saleroom on a busy street in Birkdale, Southport, to tackle the National; a selling-plater on the Flat, he had raced over ninety times by that never-to-be-forgotten day, Saturday 2 April 1977.

Red Rum had done his training on the sands of Southport just a few miles from Aintree where the sands of time have rolled in and out on a tide of emotion to the sound of hooves beating out the Grand National Story, the greatest steeplechase in the world. Long Live the National!

Right: One horse, two jockeys – Joe Guest and No Justice give John Cook a lift back to the weighing-room in 1970: No Justice had refused second time round at Becher's where Cook was brought down on Specify, but a year later Cook and Specify needed no help as they won by a neck from Black Secret

Below: Two horses, one jockey – that's the way it looks as New Zealand amateur Dennis Gray parts company with Alpenstock (34) at the fifteenth in 1979, and Purdo (5), who had fallen at the sixth, races on alone

Opposite page: First things first – Aubrey Brabazon has time for a drink and a smoke after falling at Becher's on Luan Casca in 1947

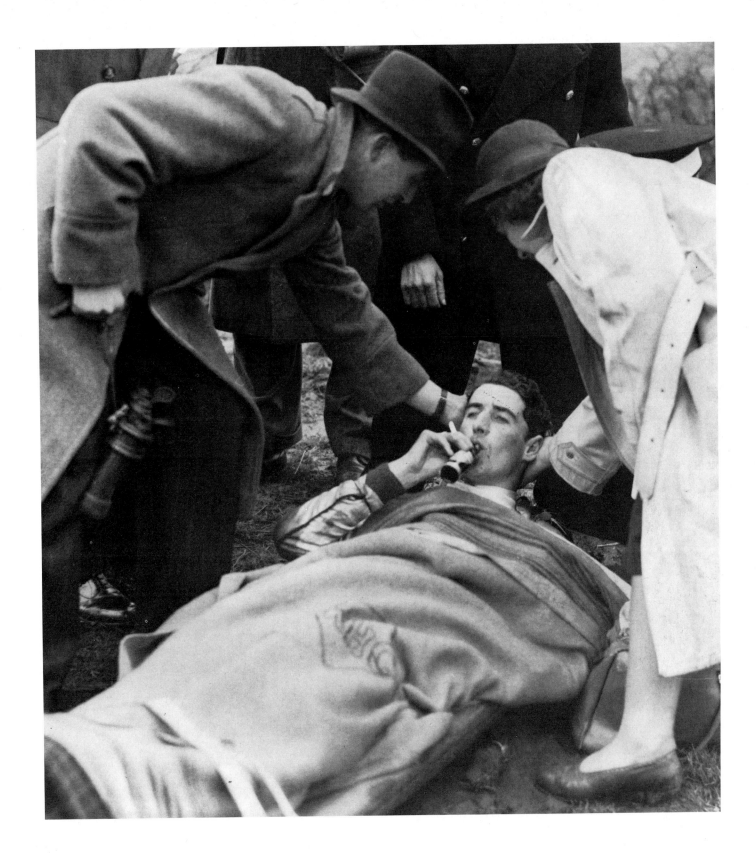

John Hughes

John Hughes in the winner's enclosure at Aintree

We met and fell in love just as so many before me, and so many since. For I share my love for the Grand National with millions all over the world. My heart flutters every time I watch these magnificent men and their courageous horses tackle the world's greatest steeplechase. The National is like no other sporting event on earth and I am proud to have been associated with it since December 1975.

It was then that Ladbrokes, with the wisdom of their chairman, Cyril Stein, signed an agreement with Aintree's owner Bill Davies to manage the racecourse and run the National for seven years, to breathe new life into this great event. And I, as Clerk of the Course employed by Ladbrokes, was to experience a series of emotions I never knew existed.

It did not take me long to realise that the National is something extra special, more than just a horse race. An event which is part of our very heritage. A race certainly which transcends all others. The National has the ability to produce the unexpected every time; to twist its tale every year and it has provided me with memories to last a lifetime.

The task of restoring the National to its rightful place in the sporting calendar in 1975 seemed, however, a daunting one. No one could ever question the event itself but Aintree had become increasingly dilapidated and the crowds, so essential to any major event, had lost interest and drifted away. Mirabel Topham had run ten 'last' Grand Nationals; Bill Davies had staged two flops and there seemed little enthusiasm from racegoers for the race. Whilst many people have been critical of Mrs Topham and her regime, it is only fair to say that she received minimal support from the racing authorities. In view of the narrow margin of profitability likely to be achieved in any one year, there was little chance of substantial money being available to modernise the stands and improve the amenities. Aintree sadly lagged far behind the majority of the country's top racecourses.

Both Flat and jumping took place at Aintree on a number of days in the late fifties and sixties but received poor support from the racing public and once it became clear to Mrs Topham that only Grand National Day could be profitable,

An electronic screen opposite the stands enabled racegoers to watch the National action all the way round for the first time in 1982

she, not unnaturally, reduced the number of fixtures. The overheads in running a course the size of Aintree are enormous and there seemed no way to arrest the slide.

To some extent the blame for falling attendances must be laid at the door of the BBC. Their television production of this compelling spectacle achieved such a remarkable quality that only a few people were willing to travel to see the National live on a course which spans such distances.

The question facing Ladbrokes, therefore, was whether income could be achieved other than through the turnstiles and whether the public could be attracted back in vast numbers. We understood that the paying crowd in 1975 was no more than 9,000.

Curiously, I felt that we should harness the appeal of television and exploit outdoor advertising which was a relatively new source of income for racing. So, in December 1975, Peter Thompson, the then Ladbrokes Marketing Director, and I set about breathing new hope into the old lady with the invaluable help of a small group of enthusiastic staff.

We fully recognised the importance of television; the amount of racing the BBC covered at the three-day National meeting would, for example, greatly affect our ability to attract sponsors. Indeed, the guarantee of television support undoubtedly enabled us to attract sponsorship for ten other races at the 1976 meeting, thus dramatically upgrading the overall programme. I must pay tribute to a host of people in the Outside Broadcast and Sports Department of the BBC and in particular to Cliff Morgan, the former Welsh rugby international, whose enthusiasm for the National as head of OB was most infectious. It became clear that the BBC's belief in the National as a sporting spectacle warranted a total investment, including operational costs, of nearly £500,000 a year.

On National Day in 1976 Aintree was alive again to the sound of thousands; 42,000 were there to see Rag Trade give Fred Rimell his record-breaking fourth National winner. For the first time, I was able to participate in the sheer joy of that special moment as the National winner is led into the winner's enclosure. The scenes never cease to amaze me and when Red Rum won in 1977, the only horse ever to win the National three times, well, I have never experienced anything like it. There were hardened racing men with handkerchiefs to their eyes just as there were four years later when Bob Champion and Aldaniti walked into the enclosure. It is hard to say which of these victories was the more compelling; sufficient to say, I have been extraordinarily fortunate to have witnessed both.

The National really gets to you like no other race – not even the Derby with all its magic compares, and I was ten years at Epsom. Perhaps it is odious to make comparisons between the two as each is so special in its own right but the incredible bravery of horse and rider sets the National apart.

It is suggested that 600 million now view the National, a clear indication of the world-wide interest in the race as a spectacle alone, for in many instances it is seen long after the result is known. This is a fact that the News Group Newspapers have not failed to recognise and led to them sponsoring the National under the banner of the *News of the World* or *The Sun* continuously since 1975, with the one exception of 1976. Their support had an undoubted effect on the revival of the race.

With responsibilities stretching in many different directions, I would find it quite impossible to single out one or two particular events. I hope, therefore, to be able to convey some overall impressions of National days from behind the scenes.

There is nothing like actually being at Aintree to savour the atmosphere, and for me, that has meant starting work at seven on National Day itself when the runners exercise on the course. Even then one begins to sense the importance of the occasion – although it is also then that things start going wrong. I know that

Aintree is silent and deserted for most of the year. But on National day it comes alive in a blaze of colour

something will always go wrong but I never have the vaguest idea what it will be. We spend a considerable amount of time during the year working on the vulnerable areas, trying to strengthen the weaknesses and anticipating the problems, but however well that work has been done, something will take me totally by surprise. You wouldn't believe the chaos that can be caused by a number board not working properly or an electric clock going wrong or a horse having to be re-shod at the start.

Police control, stable security, ambulance services, vets, the condition of the track and fences – there are a million and one things to check. For this reason, I sought assistance from other licenced Clerks of Courses and allotted specific areas of responsibility. In that respect I am most grateful to Hugo Bevan, Clerk of

Aintree in the grip of winter and the men who look after it: in the foreground is Steve Westhead, acknowledged as the course's greatest fence builder until his death shortly after the 1980 race. The third fence has been named after him

the Course at Huntingdon, Worcester and Towcester; John Williams of Hereford and Ludlow, and Rodger Farrant of Chepstow. Roderick Fabricius, a long-time colleague and one-time pupil of mine of whom I am particularly proud, undertook responsibility for general administration during Ladbrokes' reign, a daunting task considering we are operating on only a once-a-year basis.

I simply must mention a few people who have played vital roles since 1976. The important task of marketing the National has been most ably masterminded by Nigel Payne, originally in his role as Marketing Director at Ladbrokes and later under the auspices of the International Racing Bureau. Then there was the late Steve Westhead, acknowledged as the greatest fence builder; he has been succeeded as racecourse foreman by Ossie Dale, previously known to trainers from far and wide as the most welcoming, efficient and delightful stable manager. So many people in all kinds of ways have played an incredibly important part and each year it becomes a little easier and a little more efficient.

But there is always the unexpected; a demonstration by a number of people at the start one year, a red alert bomb scare another year when we had to make an immediate decision whether or not to evacuate the stands, the call in the middle of the night in 1982 to tell me a fence had been burned down – it turned out to be less serious but that call did nothing for my beauty sleep!

There is always the charisma, the fun, the camaraderie like the night before the 1979 National when I happened to stay in the same small hotel as Charlie Fenwick and his friends. We had a late night which is something I always try to avoid before the National and next day all my friends put their bets on Charlie and Ben Nevis only to get it wrong by one year.

The tension of the day mounts when the National runners go to the saddling stalls. It is an anxious time for all concerned, for owners, trainers, stable lads and lasses and, of course, the jockeys. It is no less anxious for me. It is no easy task to get the horses saddled up and into the paddock for the waiting crowds and the scene in the parade ring is, to say the least, confused with forty or so horses and at least 140 humans in a very confined area. After the last-minute instructions, the horses go out on to the course for the parade itself.

It can be difficult to get all those horses into numerical order but with one of my Stewards, Lord Grimthorpe, as ring-master, we get them sorted out before they parade in front of the stands and then go down for a look at the first fence and back to the start. It gives one a chance of a word with many of the jockeys and the response to my 'good luck' from my old friend Jonjo O'Neill is always the same: 'Well, boss [he never fails to use the word boss], it may be my turn to get round this year!' Poor Jonjo, he still has not made it.

The race itself is rather more enjoyable a couple of days later seen on the video from the comfort of my armchair. At the time, there is little chance to watch it. The concentration is inevitably on the horses, the veterinary and medical services

Pandemonium in the winner's enclosure in 1974 after Red Rum's second victory. The police had a difficult time holding back the crowds

and perhaps, above all as the race nears its end, the police control over the public. It is impossible to mention police activities without recording the role played by Constable Brian McIndoe who has been my constant shadow throughout every race day since 1978. Some people have referred to him as my bodyguard. In fact, he makes a passage through crowds, stamps out any threat of hooliganism, summons emergency services and a hundred and one other things, including taking and receiving messages for me on the police radios. Perhaps most important of all has been his direct radio contact with his colleague alongside Hugo Bevan, which has proved invaluable and never more so than when Hugo has accompanied Royalty out in the country.

It is ironic that PC McIndoe, or Brian as he has become known to me and many of my colleagues, is throughout the rest of the year a desk-waller in the Liverpool Police communications department. He claims that he covers more miles shadowing me at Aintree during the three days than he does the rest of the year. He has certainly become part of the team to the extent that it is now almost impossible to imagine the National meeting without my shadow!

The scenes in the winner's enclosure, while pretty hard to control, somehow set the seal on the whole occasion – the David Coleman interview, the historic words as the jockey slides off the horse, the frenzied greeting from the winning owner, the look of pride in the eyes of the stable lad or lass and trainer, the wild enthusiasm of the crowd.

No words of mine would be complete without a special mention of Lord Derby, my Senior Steward throughout the seven-year period from 1976. He has given me such tremendous help and encouragement and, in particular, has shielded me from unnecessary involvement in some of the minor operational technicalities which on an ordinary race day can be so very time consuming.

But then Grand National Day is no ordinary day, no ordinary race and I am delighted that so many of the leading characters in its great history have agreed to share their memories.

The Aldaniti Team

They were an unhappy team gathered around the chestnut gelding under the trees by the racecourse stables at Sandown on Friday 30 November 1979. The horse's tendon was so badly strained his fetlock joint was on the ground. 'It seemed as if the kindest thing to do would be to put him down,' recalled the trainer, Josh Gifford.

There, in the middle of the group, stood Bob Champion whose inspiration in a painful, agonising fight against cancer had been the thought of recovering and riding that very horse, Aldaniti, in the Grand National.

'When Bob was told in the summer of 1979 that he had cancer, we didn't know what to think,' said Gifford. 'As the months went by, I was convinced he would never ride again. I told him his job was always there when he was ready to come back; my heart told me he'd never make it . . .'

Champion had gone to Sandown that day to see Aldaniti take part in a race without him for the first time, to see him have his first race of the season, an ordinary enough looking affair, the 3 mile 5f Ewell Handicap Chase. Aldaniti already knew what it was like to suffer for he had been sidelined for thirteen months with tendon trouble between January 1976 and February 1977 and had another full year off the racecourse after returning lame to Gifford's stables at Findon in Sussex, following the 1977 Hennessy at Newbury on 26 November.

He had come back twice before but surely a third time was too much to ask? Champion somehow forced a smile and turned to Aldaniti's part-owner, Valda Embiricos, and said, 'Never mind, we'll just have to come back together.'

We'll just have to come back together . . . 490 days later, there into the winner's enclosure at Aintree on Saturday 4 April 1981, walked Bob Champion and Aldaniti, stars of a fairy-tale Grand National; the oh, so happy ending to a story of one man and his horse that no one could ever have dreamed up . . . for many people the greatest Grand National memory of them all.

It was, essentially, a team triumph as everyone connected with the horse insists – the team whose world seemed to have collapsed that day at Sandown.

Beryl Millam, head girl at the Barkfold Manor Stud, with Aldaniti, whom she nursed back to fitness after his breakdown

Gifford recalled the nightmare drive back to Findon: 'All I could think about was getting Aldaniti home. He must have been in agony. It was a long miserable ride and, apart from anything else, I knew Bob would be shattered. Aldaniti looked a sorry sight that night. We put on a very tight bandage and kept it on until the swelling had settled down. When he was fit enough on 13 December 1979 we loaded him up carefully and sent him back to Nick and Valda Embiricos's Barkfold Manor Stud nearby at Kirdford. I never thought I'd see him at Findon again.'

Mike Ashton, Gifford's vet who tended the horse's needs in those grim, dark days, shared Gifford's pessimism about Aldaniti's chances of running again. 'I well remember saying, "He'll make a marvellous hunter for someone." They all agreed, though Valda, I think it was, said, "But we want to run him again."'

Aldaniti was in loving hands at Barkfold Manor where the head girl Beryl Millam recalled: 'The future looked bleak. One of his already bar-fired legs was, as we had feared, very bowed and painful. As anyone who cares for horses will know, one minute you are up in the clouds, the next down in the dumps. For us, this was one of our very low times, though we knew from experience that Aldaniti was a wonderful patient. Unlike some thoroughbred horses, he was very co-operative as we had found out when he had to stand in his stable for seven months with a hind fetlock injury in the 1977–78 season.

'The damaged tendon was cold-hosed and bandaged with iced gamgee twice daily for the rest of December. Then we put on a support bandage until 14 January when Mr Ashton put Aldaniti's leg in plaster which was not removed until 12 February. During this period of confinement, Aldaniti had to be kept happy and contented. As he was such a great favourite with everyone, Margaret Phillips and Lin Wilcox who also work at Barkfold, all the Embiricos family and several local children who come to help, he had plenty of attention which he relishes, especially as most of his fans came armed with mints to which he is very partial.

'To make him so very much more comfortable, we put a heat lamp in his stable which he loved; he stood under it for ages and enjoyed the armfuls of grass that were picked for him daily as his diet was mainly of bran mashes and hay.

Josh Gifford and Aldaniti at work in Findon, Sussex. 'I decided that I would ride him in all his work,' said Gifford

'When the plaster was taken off, Mr Ashton and I smiled, I think for the first time; the leg was beautifully cool and had fined down. It was bandaged until being pin fired a week later. Aldaniti was able to be led out on to the lawn outside his stables for a bit of grass soon afterwards.

'Eventually, after eight more long weeks, Aldaniti was turned out for his summer rest which itself was not uneventful as he was plagued with foot trouble at different times in his front feet and one hind which had to be rubbed and plugged and on one occasion needed antibiotics. During this time in the field, Aldaniti was regularly wormed and had his flu jabs before being brought back to work. On the vet's advice, we left him out as long as possible.'

They got Aldaniti up on 27 October 1980. 'We left him out in our paddocks for as long as possible, the long wet grass and the autumn dew helped his legs,' explained Valda Embiricos, who picked up the story. 'He first had a saddle on him three days later and to start with I rode him for fifteen to twenty minutes each day, increasing this gradually as the days passed. He was just walked for six weeks and then we started to trot him and give him the occasional hack canter, exercising him over our nearby Bedham Hills.

'It was all road work, and would take nearly two hours, a round trip of nine miles which included a non-stop steep climb of a mile and a half. This climb made him work and he really used himself; when meeting the steepest part, he would put his head down and lengthen his stride. He is such a willing, active horse, one who never has to be kicked. We all used to ride him, myself and the team of three we have at the stables. He is a perfect gentleman and never turns a hair at the biggest or noisiest lorry passing by. Margaret Phillips used to "do" him. You could leave his stable door open, tell him not to come out and he wouldn't – except for one occasion when he had his head collar on and thought "that means action" and so wandered forth!'

One evening, Josh and his wife Althea were having dinner with Nick and Valda when Nick turned to Josh and said, 'You are going to have Aldaniti back.' Josh replied, 'Don't be silly, Nick, he'll never stand training.' But Nick insisted. 'I think he will,' he said, 'and we are going to give him a chance.'

Even then, Gifford was pessimistic. 'Okay, if you really want to,' he told Nick. 'I'd love to have him back but you are probably wasting your money.' Nick, ever the optimist, said, 'We probably are, but let's have a go. We'll go and try to win the National with him!' They all drank to that . . .

Bob Champion, meanwhile, had been fighting his own horrendous battle with cancer, though he admitted later 'Aldaniti's lameness made me give up fighting for a couple of weeks. The Grand National had been my goal, a target for me to aim at. Once Aldaniti was out, I knew I wouldn't ride again during the 1979–80 season and so gave up all hope. That was the hardest time, the closest I came to giving up.'

Findon stable lad Peter Double with his successful charge, Aldaniti

Champion, with the help of countless friends in the racing world and the staff at the Royal Marsden Hospital in Sutton, Surrey, did not give up. He battled on through the often agonising course of chemotherapy treatment and the many side effects it produced until, on 1 April 1980, he was able to fly to the United States for a three-week stay at Camden, South Carolina, as a work jockey with Burly Cocks's horses. He rode in the morning and spent the afternoons building up his muscles at the health spa. Most important of all, Bob Champion was back in the saddle.

After three weeks in Camden, Bob drove to New York where he stayed with Tommy Skiffington and during the next week, he rode at least six horses each morning at the Belmont track. Friday 30 May was the day of reckoning – Bob's first ride in public on a horse called Double Reefed in a Flat race at Fairhill, a small, undulating, grass country racecourse. It was Bob's first-ever race on the Flat; his horse was favourite – and he won. 'I couldn't really believe it was happening,' he said. 'I was blowing hard at the end of the race but not as badly as I had expected. I was chuffed to bits. I'd ridden a winner straight away and that had taken a lot of pressure off me. I thought I was a jockey again – and a Flat jockey at that!'

Bob had one more ride before returning elated to England for further medical checks. Bob Champion was back. Back on the road to Aintree . . .

It was 22 December 1980 before Aldaniti was back at Findon and into the care of stable lad Peter Double, who said: 'I was surprised like everyone else to see him back after all he'd been through. One look at his scarred legs told its own story and it seemed highly optimistic to think in terms of him ever going chasing again. Because of that, none of the lads really wanted to "do" Aldaniti at the time. Naturally, we all like to see our horses run and you couldn't hold out much hope for Aldaniti but I was a horse short at the time, so he was mine. What a stroke of luck that turned out to be! And what a marvellous horse to look after, a perfect gentleman, never a moment's bother. To tell the truth, there's nothing outstanding about him, he's like a thousand other horses in the yard with no peculiar or wayward habits. A very easy horse to look after.

'Little did I know that December that Aldaniti would change my life so dramatically, take me into a social world I'd never entered and introduce me to people I would never have met . . .'

Gifford recalled: 'I had one aim in mind – to get Aldaniti to the National. I thought we'd give him perhaps one race before, though I felt I could get him fit enough without a race if necessary so long as his legs would stand it. I decided that I would ride him in all his work. I didn't want to wrap him in cotton wool, but I just felt that if anything went wrong then I couldn't blame one of my staff.

'Our horses are fed at six o'clock and first lot go out at 7.30 – Aldaniti and I

The day after the fairy-tale National – Bob Champion, Josh Gifford and Nick Embiricos

went with them. If the string was doing faster work, I went out the back or a long way in front and just went very steadily, gradually moving on to faster work and then only if the ground was absolutely perfect for him.'

Incredibly, everything went smoothly for the Aldaniti team. Bob was back riding regularly and Aldaniti, well, it was amazing. 'I could hardly believe it,' said Gifford. 'The more work we did, the better his legs seemed to be. He was beginning to go very well and lose his tummy and it then became a question of picking the right race for him before the National.'

Nick Embiricos was getting more excited by the day – and insisted on backing Aldaniti to win the National. He was accommodated at 66–1 – and had £250 each way.

Gifford decided on the comeback race; the Whitbread Trial Handicap at Ascot on Wednesday 11 February 1981. Champion went to Findon and popped his pal over half a dozen fences and they were ready to take on seven, race-fit opponents over 3 miles and with 11st 7lb to carry. Bob went to post under strict instructions: whatever you do, bring him back in one piece.

'I suffered agonies before the race,' said Gifford, 'but once they got going I could hardly believe what I saw, it was so perfect. The horse was unbelievable; he did everything so well, jumped splendidly apart from a slight mistake at the last fence first time round, had a nice run into the straight and then took it up between the last two and absolutely cruised home by four lengths. It was more than we had dared hope for in our wildest dreams and I knew then we needn't run him again before the National.'

Aldaniti and Bob Champion were back together. 'He is one of the bravest horses I ever sat on. I was merely a passenger,' said Bob. Nick Embiricos was overjoyed – now for the National. Aldaniti did not run again before Aintree though Gifford admits he was tempted to try for the Cheltenham Gold Cup. 'I thought it was going to be a bad Gold Cup, but Nick would have none of it.'

Aldaniti was given 10st 13lb for the National, the ideal weight for Champion, whose battle with the scales was eventually to force his premature retirement in April 1982. 'It enabled me to ride on my middle saddle, my favourite one, which weighs about three pounds.'

By the day of the National, Bob Champion and Aldaniti had become the people's choice to complete their amazing story by winning the world's greatest steeplechase. He had told readers of the *Sunday People*, in a brilliant and moving interview with his great friend, journalist Jonathan Powell: 'I badly want to win the race for so many people, in particular the doctors and nurses who kept me going when all hope seemed gone. I also want to win for Josh who kept my job waiting for me and then helped me through a bad patch when my confidence was rock bottom. Few, if any, trainers would have done the same. My family, friends and many owners were terrific, too. Nick and Valda Embiricos sent me get well cards and I even had one from Aldaniti who has his own fan club organised by their daughter Alexandra.

'But most of all I want to win the Grand National for all the patients still in hospital. If any success I have can give people fresh heart and just a bit of hope then everything that has happened to me in the past twenty months will have been worthwhile.'

There were thirty-eight other jockeys sharing Bob's dream of winning; those thirty fearsome fences between his eleven-year-old partner Aldaniti and victory: but the wishes of millions went with them and a mountain of money ensured that they set off as the 10–1 second favourites to Spartan Missile and that magnificent horseman, John Thorne. The script for the race, however, must surely have been written by that great judge in the sky . . .

Aldaniti stood off too far from the first fence, flew it, but came down too steep. Champion thought they were gone. One minute Aldaniti was down, his nose and knees scraping the grass, but somehow he got back up and the partnership was in one piece. Champion hoped it had taught Aldaniti a lesson. He scraped his belly on the second – that hurt, and certainly taught him an even sharper lesson. The third, the big ditch, surprised him but Aldaniti did not flinch and after that he jumped quite brilliantly.

By the twelfth, bobbing happily along for all to see, were the white and royal blue colours of Champion and Aldaniti, his white face showing in front. Champion picks up the story as he told it in his autobiography, *Champion's Story*, so superbly chronicled by Jonathan Powell.

Out in front, Bob Champion and Aldaniti take Becher's ahead of Pacify and Steve Jobar

His superior class and jumping ability had carried him to the front sooner than anyone would have wanted. There was no point in hauling him back. I just hoped he would settle better in front . . . Aldaniti made nothing of the Chair. He saw a nice long stride, took off and really pinged it. He must have been good because all the photographs show me sitting up his neck like a Flat race jockey and you don't see that very often. He popped over the water and going out on the second circuit I tried to find the ridge of good ground in the middle of the course. Aldaniti was still running away at that stage. Rubstic was on my inside and Royal Stuart on my outside and neither of them seemed to be going as well.

I was still a bit unhappy about being in front for so long but I began to think I might have a chance of winning if I kept my head. I kept telling myself to think like a jockey and not get too excited . . .

Aldaniti was so quick away from his fences. I'd ridden at Liverpool many times but I'd never sat on anything that jumped there like Aldaniti. He was like a cat, so fast, so sure and loving every minute of it . . . but a jockey can get so wrapped up with the excitement of jumping that he forgets about

The winning post – Bob Champion and Aldaniti come home triumphant to the delight of millions

riding a race. The further we went the more I realised we might win if I didn't do anything silly. By the time we got to Becher's we were a few lengths clear . . . I kept trying to give him little breathers between the fences, to get a bit of oxygen into his lungs. His legs felt fine, he hadn't faltered at all.

Aldaniti headed back across the Melling Road, two lengths clear of Royal Mail with Spartan Missile in fifth place but making steady progress after being badly hampered at the Canal. Royal Mail, the top weight with 11st 7lb, loomed menacingly but hit the second last and nearly fell; Spartan Missile jumped the last in third place, making up ground at an astonishing pace while Aldaniti and Bob Champion made for home with Aintree in pandemonium.

When we got to the elbow, halfway up the run-in, Aldaniti had a rail to help him. He was so tired by then but he still had the strength to keep his stride unbroken. There was too much noise to hear anything but I knew something was there just behind me. You can sense it. Once I had the running rail there was still more than a furlong to go so I gave him one more crack just to make him aware that we had not finished . . .

Aldaniti kept going and by the post there were four lengths between him and the second, Spartan Missile, whose rider John Thorne sportingly rode over and clapped Bob on the back. 'A marvellous result,' said John later. 'His win is the best story this century.'

Aintree dissolved into a flood of tears; racing was a little richer and the world seemed a better place to live in for the Aldaniti team had shown us all the very acceptable face of sport. Their victory wasn't just about winning the National, it was about winning against the odds, the most incredible odds surely ever set against one man and his horse.

Neville Crump

There was a twinkle in Neville Crump's eye as he barked out, 'Sure, the Grand National changed my life; I might not have ended up so poor if I hadn't trained the Aintree winner in 1948! Suddenly I was the wonder boy and everyone wanted me to train for them, but they were all jumpers. Maybe if I'd had a decent Flat horse or two, I might have earned a few bob!'

Crump went into racing when he left the 4th Hussars in 1935 going to J. L. Hall's stable at Russley Park in Wiltshire. He started on his own in 1937 at nearby Upavon sending out sixteen winners before going back into the Army for the war. At the end of the war, he sold his stables and moved to Warwick House in Middleham, Yorkshire, and after just two years there the village tasted Grand National Triumph as Sheila's Cottage was paraded through a market square adorned with flags and bursting with pride. It was a scene repeated twice more as Crump sent out Teal (1952) and Merryman II (1960) to complete a hat-trick.

But Crump admits there is nothing like your first National winner; 20 March 1948, is etched in his memory forever and those who were there to share his triumph still laugh at the sight of him bursting through the crowds round the winner's enclosure and smacking Sheila's Cottage on the rump with the immortal words, 'Well done, you old bitch!' The old bitch flicked out a hind leg like lightning and missed Crump's head by inches . . .

'Make no mistake, Sheila's Cottage was an absolute swine, a real old brute,' recalled Crump. 'She'd bite and kick anybody but she knew what she was about on the racecourse. In fact, I let her take her chance in the 1947 National and she was going well enough until being knocked down at the twelfth. Her owner, Sir Hervey Bruce, had to sell her after she'd finished third in the 4-mile Stayers Handicap at Cheltenham the following December but I found a buyer all right – a real character, John Procter, a trawler owner who had interests in the hotel business. She ran a couple of times at Haydock and Doncaster in John's colours before the National for which she started at 50–1 in a field of forty-three; that seemed a fair reflection of her chance at the time, although I had no doubt about her ability to stay the course.

'Even so, there was no concealing my enthusiasm as they swung towards the Canal Turn on the second circuit. The winner looked sure to come from seven runners and Sheila's Cottage was among them on the inside. First of the Dandies led over Valentine's and increased his lead as he came onto the racecourse, pursued by Zahia with our horse next, resolutely galloping, just as we knew she would.

'Then came the real drama of the race as First of the Dandies jumped the second last just ahead of Zahia. That's where the horses come from the circular course on to the home straight and everyone around me gasped as Zahia and Eddie Reavey continued on the round course and out of the race. By then I could

Sheila's Cottage and Arthur Thompson win the 1948 National from First of the Dandies with Lord Mildmay back in third on Cromwell

Owner Harry lane leads in Teal and jockey Arthur Thompson after the 1952 victory with Neville Crump behind him

hardly take my eyes off Sheila's Cottage as Arthur Thompson drove her relentlessly on in pursuit of First of the Dandies, who jumped the last with a useful looking advantage.

'I turned round briefly for a word with the owner and there was John, sitting down, engrossed in a bottle of brandy. "Look here," I said, "we could win the National – aren't you interested?" He just looked up and said, "You do your job and I'll do mine; you look after the racing and I'll look after the brandy."

'And there was Sheila's Cottage eating up the ground and closing with every stride; she joined the leader 150 yards from the post and though he was tiring and bumped her, she went by him to win by a length – the first mare to win the National since Shannon Lass in 1902.

'We went back to the Adelphi that night and needless to say I didn't get home until the next day when everyone came to Warwick House and gave the horse a fabulous reception. Those were the days of some great parties at the Adelphi and they were very much part of the National itself.

'A couple of days later, a Press photographer turned up to take a picture of Sheila's Cottage with Arthur Thompson. And what did she do? She bit off the top of one of his fingers while he was trying to put on her bridle. I told him to go to the doctor but he was a tough old sod; he just got up on the horse and they got their picture.

'Arthur was also on my second National winner, Teal, in 1952. He was a splendid jockey who knew his way round Aintree backwards. He always went round the inside and liked to be up there from the start – he was the ideal man for the race.

'But Teal, well, what a crazy start he had in life. He was on offer as a two-year-old for £5 and I recall his breeder, Gerald Carroll of Co. Tipperary, saying that two prospective buyers even refused at that price. Teal was eventually sold along with another horse for £35 and one day found his way to England. Teal – or Binco as he was called at the time – was put up for sale at Stockton Sales and bought for 32 guineas but then passed from one Yorkshireman to another for four years. While Sheila's Cottage was winning at Aintree, Teal was careering round the Yorkshire moors but he finally went to Ridley Lamb of Ingleby, Barwick, who got him going. He started to win some point-to-points very impressively and a Stockton contractor Harry Lane bought him for £2,000 in May 1951.

'Harry was another character, a big man of twenty-one stone, and come Grand National Day, he chartered a train and took his wife, five daughters and six hundred of his workers to Aintree. What a day they had and my, did we celebrate! As Harry led Teal in, he threw his hat in the air and then kicked it across the unsaddling enclosure! And so would you if you'd just won the greatest steeplechase in the world and £30,000 in bets as Harry had done.

'There were some anxious moments though and Teal would surely never have won but for Arthur's magnificent riding. Teal was one of three horses to go through the tape in a breakaway which delayed the start for eleven minutes and prolonged the agony. But once they were off, Teal and Arthur were always there and thereabouts.

'But you *always* need an element of luck to win the National and Arthur had his share. Teal hit the first but got away with it; with his whip, Arthur had to ward off the riderless Caesar's Wife, who threatened disaster approaching the Chair; then Teal rapped Becher's hard, really hard, second time round. He skidded along on his belly for twenty yards with Arthur calmly sitting there, waiting for him to get to his feet. He got him up but down he went again. Arthur stayed perfectly still and Teal recovered. The incident had allowed Freebooter to take the lead with Legal Joy third and my other runner, Wot No Sun, fourth. Teal was back in front by the Canal Turn where Freebooter fell and it looked a three horse-race between Teal, the improving Royal Tan and Legal Joy.

'Teal and Legal Joy jumped the last together with Royal Tan trying to close but Royal Tan fell leaving Teal to wear down Legal Joy, who was ridden by Michael Scudamore, and go on and win by five lengths. Arthur put it all down to a good luck charm he had received from his sister in Ireland – a small cross which he put in his breeches and it went round Aintree with him.

'Sadly, luck was never again on Teal's side. He died a few months later from a twisted gut leaving me to reflect on what might have been, for I shall always think that Teal would have won the 1953 Cheltenham Gold Cup.

'I've certainly been lucky with my jockeys and Gerry Scott, who rode my third National winner Merryman II in 1960 was another brilliant horseman. Mind you, he shouldn't have even ridden in that race let alone anything else. Gerry had a double-fracture of the collar-bone but I persuaded an Irish doctor the night before to let him ride – they'd never let anyone go out there in that condition these days!

'Merryman II almost didn't make it either. After running at Chepstow the previous December, he was so lame that I had to send him for two days to the Edinburgh Veterinary Hospital where they diagnosed a severely bruised pedal bone. I turned him out with a rug on him and about two days before the forfeit stage I got him in, but he was still lame. We put shoes on him and walked him round and suddenly he was as sound as a bell.

'I first saw Merryman II winning the Buccleuch Hunters Chase by twenty lengths at Kelso in April 1958, the first time he had run under National Hunt rules. I never stopped badgering his owner, Miss Winifred Wallace, to let me train him. Miss Wallace hunted him and won three point-to-points on him before sending him to me.

'From the moment he won the Liverpool Foxhunters Chase at Aintree in March 1959, I felt he would win me my third National. He never made a single mistake on his introduction to Aintree, going clear at Becher's when ridden by amateur Charlie Scott. He followed up by winning at Bogside in April and then Gerry Scott (no relation to his previous partner) rode him to victory in the Scottish Grand National by twelve very impressive lengths.

'I decided to give him only four races before the National and though he didn't win any, he started 13–2 favourite for the big race in a field of twenty-six – and ran out the first clear favourite to win since Sprig in 1927. The bookies took a caning that day for Mustavon, who was also trained in Middleham by Sam Hall, had won the Lincoln on the previous Wednesday and been coupled extensively with Merryman II.

'We had just two anxious moments. Merryman II landed on his head at Becher's both times round and Gerry really thought he'd gone the second time but the horse somehow staggered to his feet again and stormed on to win by fifteen lengths from Stan Mellor on Badanloch.

'The two fought a lone dual from Valentine's second time round but Merryman II gave Gerry a magnificent ride, jumping brilliantly and never really looking as though he would be beaten. I was thrilled for Gerry who had been with

Teal was one of three horses to break through the tape in a false start to the 1952 National, which delayed the race for eleven minutes

Left: Teal leads Legal Joy over the last on the way to victory in 1952, with Royal Tan just approaching the fence

Right: Winifred Wallace leads in Merryman II and Gerry Scott in 1960; this was trainer Neville Crump's third National winner

me right from the age of sixteen, six years earlier. It was only his second ride in the National.

'There is no doubt that Merryman II was the best Liverpool horse I have trained – one of the few greats, although Teal may have been generally more brilliant. I really don't know whether Merryman II would have beaten Teal, but I'm bound to say both would have beaten Sheila's Cottage.

'I remain convinced, however, that Merryman II would have won again the following year. He was kicked so severely on the stifle by Jimuru at the start that it was touch and go whether he would have to be withdrawn. However, he took part – with Derek Ancil riding him because Gerry was injured. Merryman II put up a tremendous effort, half-lame and ridden by an unfamiliar jockey and carrying 11st 12lb, a stone more than he had carried to victory, to finish second, beaten only five lengths by Nicolaus Silver, who was getting nearly two stone.'

Now, more than twenty years later, Crump looks with affection and pride at the pictures on the wall of his Middleham home of the three horses who changed his life and set him out on a road that has made him one of the country's most successful National Hunt trainers.

Tim Forster

Tim Forster

Bowgeeno, Tim Forster's first Grand National runner, had finished fourth to Specify in 1971 when the Letcombe Bassett trainer visited one of his owners, Heather Sumner, in hospital. 'Don't worry,' she told Tim, 'we'll win it next year with Well To Do.'

Mrs Sumner died shortly afterwards leaving Tim the choice of her five horses. 'I had no hesitation in choosing Well To Do,' recalled Tim. 'He was Mrs Sumner's favourite horse and I had bought him with her for 750 guineas as an unbroken three-year-old from Mrs Hugh Lloyd Thomas, whose late husband had owned the 1937 National winner Royal Mail. Therefore I followed his racing life right through; nobody else had ever handled him, touched him or had anything to do with him.'

And Heather Sumner was proved right when, on 8 April 1972, Well To Do won the National. 'Sentiment very seldom pays off in racing, but for once it had in a big way,' recalled Tim, who admits even now that he almost had cold feet and never ran the horse.

'I suppose I was frightened that something might happen to him and I did have a few misgivings. Indeed, I only declared him for the race fifteen minutes before the entries closed! The remark Mrs Sumner had made to me in hospital finally convinced me he should run though I discussed the situation fully with her family.'

The decision made, Forster then found himself more bullish about Well To Do's prospects than any other race in his life. 'Everyone knows what a pessimist I am,' mused the Old Etonian as he fitted his six-foot frame into an armchair and re-lived that first Aintree triumph, 'but I can genuinely say that a week before the National, for some extraordinary reason, the horse was better than he'd ever been in his life, before or afterwards. I wouldn't have dared tell anyone at the time but I felt, given ordinary luck and without any drama or accident, Well To Do *would* win the National.

'I knew he jumped exceptionally well, he stayed forever and, in Graham Thorner, he was being ridden by a top-class jockey. I'd never had the horse better; I think it was just luck but Well To Do is the only horse I've ever run anywhere in the world where I felt that way.'

Forster's enthusiasm was fired by a piece of work a week before Aintree. 'I can only gallop seven furlongs here, so Well To Do had a long canter round a great big field for about a mile and a half and then quickened up for seven furlongs; he was just running away the whole time, pulling hard which he never usually did. He was normally lazy and wouldn't take hold of his bridle when he was working. This particular morning, I'd never seen anything like it. I just knew he was completely right.'

All the signs seemed right – even the stars seemed to be on Forster's side as he opened a newspaper on National morning and read his Pisces horoscope: 'You'll be sharing secrets, doing a lot of planning this weekend. Good weekend for sport.' Good weekend for sport, indeed! It was a weekend Forster will never forget . . .

Well To Do, carrying just 10st 1lb – 'the perfect weight for him, just right' – jumped like a buck the whole way round. Thorner, who had been with Forster since leaving school in 1964, went the shortest way on the inside and as they came to the second last, four of the forty-two runners were in with a chance.

'I'd managed to get up on the roof,' recalled Forster, 'and I kept thinking it was going to collapse and what a horrible way that would be to go! I remember seeing Well To Do come to the last and thinking, "I don't believe it, I can't believe it." And then halfway up the run-in, I thought, "Oh, my God, it's that bloody Biddlecombe on Gay Trip who's challenging him, anybody but Biddlecombe, oh, no!" And hoping upon hope that he wouldn't catch him.'

Then it was over. Well To Do won by a couple of lengths with Black Secret and General Symons locked together in third place a further three lengths away. Gay Trip, winner in 1970 when Pat Taaffe rode him, had bravely fought to hump 11st 9lb through driving wind and pouring rain, but it was Well To Do's day and Forster was the first owner-trainer to win the National since Major Noel Furlong with Reynoldstown in 1935 and '36.

'Suddenly I had this terrible feeling of sadness that Mrs Sumner hadn't lived to see it,' said Forster. 'Thrilled as I was at winning the National, I couldn't help reflecting how cruel life can be; just one more year and she'd actually have been watching her own horse. I was in tears of joy and sadness at the same time.' Forster watched the race with the late Mrs Sumner's husband, John, who today has Well To Do at home with him at Marston St Lawrence.

'There was one other amazing aspect of that National,' said Forster, 'and that was the effect it had on Well To Do. I really felt for him after the race; I was worried how he'd cope with having to go through the next few weeks with people wanting to come and see him and photograph him and fuss him for he'd been a very nervous horse. The National actually changed his character, he grew up and

Well To Do and Graham Thorner get away from The Chair smartly

never looked back. He'd always left a lot of his feed after every race and the only time he ate everything was following the National. He used to strike into himself and cut himself in nearly every race yet he never had a scratch or a mark on him from the National. So as far as I'm concerned, it's nonsense to say that the National is too exhausting for a horse or that it verges on being cruel or anything like that.'

That wonderful weekend is etched in Forster's memory for ever. 'The Sunday was a marvellous day. When you're lucky enough to live and train in a village as opposed to a training centre, everyone feels it's their horse; they've seen him in the mornings, they've talked of nothing else in the weeks before the National and, of course, they've all had their two bobs on him! That's the pleasing thing, everybody locally gets so much pleasure from a win like that. It's really very touching the number of people who write to you and send telegrams, people you've never heard of perhaps since school. People write such exceptionally nice letters saying things like, "I remember you when you were riding at the Pony Club", that sort of thing.

Graham Thorner and Well To Do receive a welcome fit for a king at Letcombe Bassett the day after their 1972 triumph as the village turn out to greet them

'About a month after winning the National, I was emotionally drained; so many people had brought back so many memories; my adrenalin had been going and going and suddenly I felt totally exhausted.'

Exhausted maybe, but ready for the next time. Forster has been lucky; there has not been a next time for most trainers fortunate enough to win a National. But just eight years later, Forster was in the winner's enclosure again at Aintree with Ben Nevis. 'The horse had been coughing and there's no doubt that I wouldn't have run him if it hadn't been for the fact that his owner and rider lived in the States and the whole shooting match was on its way over,' said Forster, 'but then that's another story!' Another fascinating piece of National folklore – Charlie Fenwick's story . . .

Ginger McCain

Ginger McCain

'The National has this magic about it. Horses off the bottom of the handicap can come up and win, the little man running a small stable can come up and win; that's what makes it special, that's what makes it different.'

The owner and occupier of 10 Upper Aughton Road, Birkdale in Lancashire, was speaking and, for all his six-feet plus frame, he was one such little man in the world of racing until 31 March 1973 when he introduced us to a polished-mahogany gelding with tea-brown eyes and marvellously sensitive ears who goes by the name of Red Rum.

Donald 'Ginger' McCain will never forget that day at Aintree when Red Rum won his first National and, in doing so, sliced an incredible 19 seconds off the great Golden Miller's 39-year-old record by covering the four miles and 856 yards in 9 minutes 1.9 seconds.

Few people south of Aintree had ever heard of McCain who trained his tiny string on the sands of Southport and housed his horses in antique stables at the back of his car showrooms – and still does. Red Rum made sure racing will never forget Ginger. He returned to Aintree for the next four Nationals and became the only horse ever to win the race three times. Who could ever forget the scenes on 2 April 1977 as 51,000 people roared Rummy home and into a place in history.

Look first at his record . . .

1973 **First** carrying 10st 5lb
1974 **First** carrying 12st
1975 **Second** carrying 12st
1976 **Second** carrying 11st 10lb
1977 **First** carrying 11st 8lb

Then listen to Ginger, the man who made the horse which became everyone's favourite animal, and whose intelligent face became better known than any other sportsman or sportswoman in the country . . .

'My thoughts often wander back to my childhood, and a day in 1939. We were staying with an aunt who lives at Crosby, and on National Sunday we walked

Red Rum and his lad Billy Ellison on the sands of Southport before Rummy's first tilt at the race he was to make his own. Glenkiln, Ginger McCain's other entry in the 1973 race, follows him with The Tunku behind

beside the canal to Aintree. It was my first visit to the place. I remember there were barges drawn up along the canal banks with tiers and tiers of seats on them – five or six tiers high. There was a real carnival atmosphere, with all kinds of characters – Prince Monolulu, someone in a box with a man sticking swords through it, fire-eaters; all kind of things going on.

'Being a boy of eight or nine, and very impressionable, it stuck in my mind. I remember, too, walking back along the canal and how tired we all were; it had been quite a day. I saw my first National that year when Workman, ridden by Tim Hyde, won. At the end of the race, there were horses coming in from what seemed like miles and miles out in the country, sometimes ridden by two jockeys, sometimes even by three. Or one jockey leading two horses. It seemed to go on for hours afterwards. I know it wasn't that long really, but that was a boy's impression. That's Liverpool to me – and for me, there's never been anything else on earth.

'You will appreciate therefore that when I started training in 1969, my aim in life was to have a horse good enough to run well in the National and, who knows, maybe even win.

'From the word go, I always thought that horse might be Red Rum. I'd long since made up my mind what my ideal Aintree horse was like – not too bold at the fences because the big fences find the bold horses out; the bold horses having a real cut at the fences either burn themselves out or stand off too far at one and pay the penalty. No, I think you need a real professional, a clever horse, one who will relax in the early part of the race. I don't think shape or conformation matters at all, horses of all shapes and sizes have won the National, but you want one with courage, one who will battle on when everything else has gone.

'We were all lit up about Red Rum when he came to our yard in August 1972. We'd paid 6,000 guineas for him at the Doncaster Bloodstock Sales, six times more than we'd paid for any other horse bar one, and for a little yard like ours that was something special anyway. He was soon repaying us, however, by winning his first five races in owner Noel le Mare's colours. This was one of the many remarkable things about Red Rum – he'd been running flat out since his two-year-old days; he was even gambled on for his first two-year-old race, and it says much for his constitution.'

That first race was a 5-furlong seller on 7 April 1967 at Liverpool of all places and Red Rum was bought in by Tim Molony, the first of his five trainers, for 300 guineas after dead-heating for first place!

'By the time the 1973 National came round,' recalled Ginger McCain, 'I was obviously still really feeling my way and I also ran another horse, Glenkiln, my first runners in the race. Glenkiln had won at Aintree the previous autumn but Rummy, who had never run in a chase there, set off joint favourite at 9–1 with Crisp, who was trained by Fred Winter – the man they called Mr Grand National.

The dawning of National day and Aintree comes alive to the sound of horses. *Right*: L'Escargot and Tommy Carberry take a look at the course before their 1975 triumph. *Below*: Some of the 1976 National runners warm up for the big day

Jonjo O'Neill, incidentally, rode Glenkiln but they fell at The Chair.

'The race was one of the most exciting of all Nationals and with a fence to go, Crisp was an amazing fifteen lengths in front of Red Rum and looked sure to win. But Rummy was receiving almost 2st from him and he caught Crisp in the last few strides, winning by three-quarters of a length. It was all too much to take in; even now, it's impossible to describe my feelings. I remember though coming down from the stand and legging across the tarmac with seven league boots on, and hearing some fellow shouting and hollering and thinking, "Who's that silly bugger?" Then I thought, "It's you, you fool!"'

That was the start of a long and beautiful love affair between Rummy and racing. Each autumn, he'd bowl around a couple of northern courses, put his hooves up for the winter, then, with a spring in his step, make for Aintree and the National. 'I was lucky, of course,' said McCain, 'to have such a wonderful owner. He was only interested in Liverpool and left everything to me. He never interfered and I think the horse gave him tremendous pleasure at a time in his life when age was catching up with him and he could no longer play his game of golf, for example.' Mr le Mare was eighty-five when Red Rum won his first National.

Nothing – not even a crushing 12st – could stop Rummy again in 1974 but that long run-in beat him the following two years as McCain's miracle horse tried for an immortal hat-trick. First, L'Escargot took full advantage of his 11lb weight concession to beat Red Rum by fifteen lengths before Rag Trade, who was receiving 12lb, beat him by two lengths in 1976. And so to 2 April 1977, the day of days.

'That was a special victory, a vintage one. All the victories were marvellous, of course, but to win a third National, to do something that's never been done before, that's really something. And yet, in a way, it was the one we expected most of all. We were more confident of winning that day than on any other. Everybody, it seemed, wanted it to happen – and it did. We were so confident, it was ridiculous. The horse had so much presence that year, it was uncanny really. We'd had the sweetest run-up to the National, no problems at all, and Rummy was completely relaxed. Tommy Stack said as they walked round at the start that he'd never sat on a horse which gave him quite such a feel. He was out of this world, said Tommy, walking around as though he owned the place. He was there to do his job and he knew it.

'I had just one nagging doubt, that was all. I wondered whether we were a week short in our preparation. As it turned out we were spot on.

'Brian Fletcher had ridden him in his first three Nationals but Tommy had been on board in 1976 and he gave him a great ride this time. There were several early casualties and eleven of the forty-two runners had departed by the third fence. Two more went at the fourth as Sebastian V blazed away in front but he came down at Becher's with Castleruddery while Winter Rain tragically broke his

Opposite: The day Red Rum became the first horse to win the National three times. *Above*: The scene in the paddock before the race on 2 April 1977; John Hughes, with a police escort, directs his organization by walkie-talkie. *Below*: Red Rum and Tommy Stack all ready to go

Left: Red Rum and Tommy Stack are foot perfect at Becher's in 1977

Below left: Tommy Stack salutes the cheers that ring out for Red Rum's historic third victory in 1977

Below: The crowds flock to pay homage to a great horse

neck; that left Boom Docker in front. Prince Rock tried to stop at the ditch before coming back on to the racecourse for the first time and sent Graham Thorner flying over it ahead of him. Then Boom Docker's lead was increased still further when Sage Merlin, who had been leading the pursuers, came to grief at The Chair.

'That left Andy Pandy second, ahead of Brown Admiral, What A Buck, Sir Garnet, Forest King, Nereo, Happy Ranger, Sandwilan and The Pilgarlic with Rummy not far behind them, with Churchtown Boy and Eyecatcher beginning to improve. Boom Docker ground to a halt at the first fence on the second circuit leaving Andy Pandy in command. He stayed there until Becher's where he was ten lengths clear – but crumpled on landing. Nereo also came down with Brown Admiral and Saucy Belle, who was remounted, while Sandwilan pulled up.

'And who was out in front? Yes, Rummy, with more than a mile and eight fences to go. Daft as it sounds now, we never had any bones about the race; we somehow knew we'd win, and apart from a couple of loose horses worrying Rummy at the Canal Turn, it was all plain sailing from there on in. Churchtown Boy, who had won the Topham Trophy on the Thursday, made a mistake at the second last and Rummy went further and further away from him to win by an incredible twenty-five lengths.

Injury forced Red Rum out of the 1978 race at the last minute, but he still stole the show as he paraded in front of the packed stands

'Tommy Stack had it right when he said after the race, "Nothing can do justice to this horse, nothing I can say and nothing anyone can write; he is just beyond belief."

'It was, it was just beyond belief. Bloody marvellous! Bloody marvellous on Tommy's part and bloody marvellous on the horse's part!

'And he'd have gone close to winning it again the following year, too – if he'd run. Everything was perfect until one week before the race when I sensed something was wrong by the way he was using himself behind. I thought at the time, the old bugger's starting to get a touch of arthritis. After all, he was thirteen, he was entitled to. Apart from anything else, he'd jumped 150 fences round Aintree without once falling and that's enough to take it out of anyone.

'We took him to Liverpool and worked him on the course on the Friday before the 1978 National. He worked so well that the boy had to aim him at a fence in order to pull him up. He couldn't anchor the horse. But Rummy wasn't right. I think now it may have been a hairline fracture of a bone in the foot; there are so many minute bones in the foot, who can say otherwise. We never really got to the bottom of it. But we decided not to run and he went out in style, leading the parade, though wondering, I'm sure, why he wasn't taking part. But he'd kept everybody on tenterhooks right to the end, wondering whether he'd run or not. I think he went out on the right note.'

And McCain, one of the little men now walking tall through life, sounded off on this note: 'To me, the National is the greatest race in the world bar none. You can talk about your Flat races or Cheltenham Gold Cups or anything, but they don't compare with the National. It's a magnificent sporting spectacle which brings out the best in a man and a horse. It is the climax of any horseman's career.'

Vincent O'Brien

Vincent O'Brien lit up the tiny, historic Tipperary country town of Cashel in three successive years with an immortal hat-trick of Grand National victories. The Irish were happy with one win in those days, and two, well that was really special – but three, and three in a row at that, was unbelievable! Impossible.

But O'Brien, who had already won three consecutive Cheltenham Gold Cups with Cottage Rake (1948–1950) and three consecutive Champion Hurdles with Hatton's Grace (1949–1951) before Early Mist won at Aintree in 1953, has scaled heights others could not reach.

He took over Ballydoyle with its 320 acres of rich, rolling parkland in 1951 and transformed it into the finest private training centre in the world. Ballydoyle, just five miles out of Cashel on the Clonmel Road, is every trainer's dream come true. In the early days, O'Brien built schooling fences and hurdles up the slope bordering the drive to the Georgian house and dreamed his Aintree dream – his dream of winning the world's greatest steeplechase.

He very nearly did that immediately in 1951 but Royal Tan made a bad mistake at the final fence and although Vincent's brother 'Phonsie' brilliantly scrambled back into the saddle when all seemed lost, they failed by six lengths to peg back Nickel Coin ridden by Johnny Bullock. Royal Tan looked even more sure to win the following year – but this time came down at the last, leaving Neville Crump's Teal to win. But 1953 was Vincent O'Brien's year, the start of the impossible dream . . .

'I went to the dispersal sale in 1952 of the late James V. Rank's horses and outbid Lord Bicester for Early Mist, an eight-year-old at the time, who had fallen at the first fence in the 1952 National. I bought him on behalf of Joe Griffin, a young Dublin businessman who had only recently come into racing.

'Early Mist caused me some concern at first for he was not a natural jumper and relied largely on his jockey to make up his mind for him. I decided that Bryan Marshall would be the ideal partner for him but, even so, he only sat on the horse once before the National when they jumped just two fences. But that was sufficient for Bryan to form the opinion that Early Mist was a hesitant sort and agree that he would have to do his thinking for him. Bryan did exactly that at Aintree and the horse responded brilliantly.

'The field of thirty-one was the smallest for the National since the war and by the time they reached Becher's on the second circuit, Early Mist was a couple of lengths in front of Mont Tremblant, the previous year's Cheltenham Gold Cup winner, with the favourite Little Yid, another couple of lengths away in third and the rest nowhere.

'Little Yid began to tire and was eventually pulled up four from home but Mont Tremblant, who was giving Early Mist 17lb, kept battling away. He actually came up to our horse's tail as they came back on to the racecourse but Bryan had things well under control and Early Mist ran on gloriously to win by twenty lengths.

'Bryan's main problem was maintaining Early Mist's concentration between the last two fences as by then he'd been out in front for a while and had started to look about him.' No doubt he was wondering why all those Irishmen were cheering like crazy!

'Early Mist was still green but to illustrate just what kind of horse he was, he had enough in him to shy at a piece of paper after passing the winning post. He jumped well and Valentine's was the only fence where he stood back a bit far and brushed the fence.

'Ironically, Early Mist won the Grand National for Joe Griffin who had only just come into racing, while his previous owner James Rank had tried all his life to win the race, without success. Yet twelve months later, Joe Griffin, Bryan Marshall and I were back in the same spot, this time with Royal Tan who had gone so agonisingly close in those two earlier attempts. I am bound to say that, of all the winners I have ever trained, Royal Tan's triumph holds a special affection for me.

'Royal Tan had developed tendon trouble after the National in 1952 and this necessitated a long rest and he did not race again until October 1953. Due to this prolonged and enforced lay-off, he had become more than usually lazy.

'Without doubt, however, he was the best natural jumper I trained and I was very perplexed when Bryan parted company with him at Gowran Park in the January before the National. It seemed horse and rider were not getting on together; but my brother, Phonsie, came up with the answer. He felt that Royal Tan was such a good and natural jumper that he did not want a jockey dictating to him. Whereas Bryan had been able to gather up Early Mist and present him at his fences, Royal Tan had to be left to jump exactly as he wished. The jockey had to sit still and leave it to the horse. Probably Royal Tan's two errors at the last fence in earlier Nationals had been due to a very understandable anxiety on Phonsie's part to get the horse over the last obstacle.

'Bryan returned to ride Royal Tan in a school over fences at Gowran Park and

Above left: Early Mist and Bryan Marshall clear the final fence on the way to victory in 1953

Above right: The magnificent Bryan Marshall and Royal Tan (2) hold off George Slack and Tudor Line for victory in 1954

Opposite page: Vincent O'Brien leads in Early Mist

rode him as Phonsie suggested. He came back, smiling, confident that we'd found the answer to the problem. Royal Tan had shown great reluctance in travelling to Liverpool two years earlier and I decided not to send him straight there. Instead, I installed him twenty miles away at Haydock and he made the short trip to the racecourse on the morning of the race.

'This time, everything went perfectly for Royal Tan – after a scare at the first when he was almost brought down by another of my runners, Alberoni! I must admit, however, I held my breath as he approached the last in the lead after passing Tudor Line between the last two. Bryan sat still over the last as we had agreed and the horse jumped perfectly whereas Tudor Line, who had a special bit to stop him jumping to the right, still jumped right.

'Even so, what a battle George Slack and Bryan had to the finish. George somehow got Tudor Line going again and they slowly, relentlessly, closed the gap. Thankfully Royal Tan and Bryan were equal to them and the old horse battled on to win by a neck; but who could deny him victory after all the earlier disappointment.

'It had been sixty-nine years since a jockey had ridden the National winner in consecutive years, and the last occasion an owner had won in successive years with different horses was 1912 and 1913 when Sir Charles Assheton-Smith won with Jerry M and Covertcoat.

'I sent four horses to Aintree the following year with Bryan electing to ride Early Mist. Dave Dick took over on Royal Tan, Fred Winter rode Oriental Way and I chose Pat Taaffe for Quare Times, who had won the 4-mile National Hunt

Above: At home at Ballydoyle, left to right: Dermot O'Brien, Major W. H. E. Welman, Vincent O'Brien and Mrs Welman (the owner) admire Quare Times with Pat Taaffe in the saddle

Opposite top: Royal Tan and Bryan Marshall (2) are almost brought down after the first in 1954 by stable companion Alberoni

Opposite below: Quare Times and Pat Taaffe complete Vincent O'Brien's National hat-trick

Chase at the Cheltenham Festival meeting in 1954.

'I had the four jockeys into my hotel sitting-room the night before the race where we looked at films of previous Grand Nationals and, as usual, I advised each of them to set off on the outside. I always felt the chances of escaping trouble from loose horses were better on the outside for the fallers inevitably went towards the inside where there were no rails and naturally veered that way to avoid jumping the fences in front of them.

'There was a torrential downpour during the night and rain continued all morning. However, it was decided to run though the water jump was railed off and dolls were erected to restrict the width of the second-last fence. The going was very heavy but Quare Times made light of it and never put a foot wrong. Once again, we had Tudor Line back in second place though there was no need for Pat to ride a finish for there were twelve lengths between first and second.'

The scenes in Ireland the next day were out of this world. Quare Times was paraded through the streets and given a civic reception in Dublin. There were bonfires everywhere and the Rock of Cashel was lit up as the horse passed through the town on the way home to Ballydoyle.

Quare Times had completed for O'Brien arguably the finest of all training achievements in the Grand National, three consecutive wins with three different horses. Though O'Brien was represented in several more Nationals – Royal Tan was third to ESB in 1956 – he gradually cut back his National Hunt string and by the sixties he was achieving the impossible on the Flat; but then, that's O'Brien.

Peter Beckwith-Smith

Major Peter Beckwith-Smith's eight-year spell as Clerk of the Course at Aintree from 1949 spanned an exciting but often controversial period in the history of the National but one that was certainly never dull as the legendary Mirabel Topham fought to preserve the great race.

'She often felt she was a lone fighter for the preservation of the National,' said Major Beckwith-Smith. 'She would say to me that she was standing on her head to keep the National going. I know she felt she had little help in the mid-fifties from the National Hunt committee and the secretariat.

'She felt that everybody was busy being unhelpful towards Liverpool. There was always this urge to alter the National course and, for example, to put in another fence after the last to reduce the length of the run-in. There was continually a delegation of pressmen and trainers saying it was ridiculous to have such a long run-in and ridiculous to have a fence like the Canal Turn. Well, maybe it is but that is part of the National, its very individuality is what has made it the great race it undoubtedly is.

'I once received a letter saying the brook at Becher's should be filled in otherwise the conditions of the race would not be published in the Racing Calendar. There were people who had nothing to do with Liverpool who went round suggesting the fences should be remade of birch and that thorn should not be used.

'Mrs Topham was a fighter on behalf of the National. She believed in the race and felt that many people failed to understand her. There's no doubt that she understood and cared deeply for the race. Her diligence laid the foundation for the splendid condition of the turf; she was always walking round or, in later years when her health began to fail, being driven round the course making sure everything was just so. The course was never neglected. I appreciate the state of the buildings is another matter but that was, in any case, a question of finance.'

Beckwith-Smith chuckled at the memory of mighty Mirabel. 'I spent hours with her trying to get her to comply with the Rules of Racing; it was rather like a game of chess. She would be absolutely charming and her hospitality was

Major Peter Beckwith-Smith

splendid but we'd talk about any and every thing except what I had gone to discuss!'

The man who was later to run Epsom and with it take responsibility for the Derby, formed a great affection for Liverpool and the National in particular. Beckwith-Smith's eight years embraced, of course, the Devon Loch disaster in 1956 when the Queen Mother's horse slumped to the ground yards from the winning post with the race won.

'That was the most dramatic incident I have ever seen and I have vivid but sad memories of that day.' Many theories have been presented for Devon Loch's collapse but Beckwith-Smith has no doubt in his mind.

'We had very big crowds in those days and they were shouting and cheering in a way that one could not imagine, absolutely thrilled that the Queen Mother was about to win the National. The horse was obviously tiring but I think there was another far more realistic factor – quite simply the noise. Devon Loch wasn't like a police horse, for example, trained to accept such noise. The sound cascades down from the stands at Liverpool in a frightening way; the stands are very upright almost perpendicular and at ground level one can almost have a claustrophobic feeling. Devon Loch must have wondered what was happening. If only one could have got on to the loudspeaker at the moment and told the crowd, "For God's sake, don't cheer!"

'Instead of being a happy day, it was a sad, bitterly disappointing one. And visions went through my mind that the water jump had leaked or there was a hole in the course and that it was entirely the fault of the Clerk of the Course.'

The Royal colours were carried in the 1950 National – Beckwith-Smith's first – for the first time since King Edward VII's death in 1910 when Monaveen, owned jointly by Queen Elizabeth and Princess Elizabeth, was among the forty-nine-horse field but he lost his chance by blundering badly at the fence before The Chair though he finished fifth and only seven completed the course. That race was won, however, by Freebooter, who carried 11st 11lb and won by fifteen lengths from Wot No Sun.

Freebooter was, as Beckwith-Smith said, 'a real Aintree horse, for besides the National he won the Champion Chase, the Grand Sefton twice, once with 12st 7lb, and The Becher also carrying 12st 7lb.' That National also marked the last appearance of Lord Mildmay, on Cromwell, before his tragic death by drowning.

Beckwith-Smith's Nationals were dominated by Vincent O'Brien – 'a truly magnificent trainer, brilliant at his profession' – who won three years in a row from 1953. 'But the 1955 race would never have taken place but for Lord Sefton,' said Beckwith-Smith.

'That was the wettest week Liverpool had ever had and I remember lying in bed at the Adelphi Hotel listening to the rain teeming down. I'd never heard such rain – and it was still pouring when I went to the course at 7.30 on Grand

Freebooter leads from Teal, the eventual winner, at Becher's on the second circuit in 1952.

National morning. Things looked hopeless. The whole place was virtually awash and one didn't know where to begin or where to look. I knew that members of the Royal Family were coming up to Liverpool and knew, too, that they would already be on their way by train.

'I rang Lord Sefton, the Senior Steward, who lived close by and said, "I don't know what we are going to do but the whole of Aintree is under water." "Yes, I know," he said, "I've lived here all my life and I've never seen seagulls floating on my lawn before. But it's too late now. Come what may, snow, ice, rain, whatever, we race."

'It was decided to omit the water jump but, even so, there were many people who felt the National should not go ahead. Lord Sefton was a very good Steward and he had all the jockeys in and told them to ride sensibly according to the

Splashing through the mud in 1955, when many people felt the race should not have gone ahead

conditions. "Any nonsense," he said, "and this could be the end of the National." The fences hadn't been altered at that time and in those days there was a lot of pressure from the RSPCA to stop the National.

'What happened? Thirteen out of thirty starters finished – the most since 1948 – and Lord Sefton's decision was entirely vindicated. I can see him now, standing outside the weighing-room with a large cigar in his hand as people went up and apologised for questioning his decision. "Apology accepted," he roared!

'Certainly Vincent O'Brien was delighted with the decision to race for it enabled him to achieve something quite remarkable in the long history of the race. He always seemed to be in the winner's enclosure – and he's been there at Epsom after a few Derbys, too!'

Beckwith-Smith left Aintree in 1957 for Hurst Park but was persuaded by Mrs

Opposite above: They're off on the world's greatest steeplechase. *Below*: John Oaksey is down, departing from Royal Relief in 1975

Topham to 'have one over the eight' in 1974 after the course had been sold to Bill Davies.

'That was my last recollection of her, and what a recollection! I was to discover that finding out what belonged to whom was extremely difficult. I went into the weighing-room to see that the Stewards Room was properly equipped with tables and chairs and that there was hot water for the valets and jockeys so they could have showers. Everything was working well and all seemed to be in apple pie order.

'However, I returned two days later and, to my horror, everything had vanished. All the furniture had been removed and a man came in and said there was no hot water or coal. I went over to Mrs Topham and told her the furniture had been removed and asked what was going on. "Oh," she said, "that belongs to the Tophams. It isn't included in the sale. The coal comes out of my house." It was too silly really but I think Mr Davies had to bring in the local haberdasher and furniture supplier to fix up the Stewards Room. I think we obtained the keys of the coal cellar from Jimmy Bidwell-Topham; certainly the jockeys had their showers!'

Life with Mirabel Topham, life with the National, life with Aintree was never dull for Major Peter Beckwith-Smith . . . 'and I wouldn't have missed it for the world.'

Jim Bidwell-Topham

Jim Bidwell-Topham: he preferred to remain an anonymous figure behind the scenes on race days

Opposite: Down and down they go – the drop at Becher's

'Royal Mail wins Royal National' declared the sporting headlines on the day following Jim Bidwell-Topham's first visit to Aintree as a boy in 1937 and he has a lasting souvenir in the shape of a gold-embossed suede racecard cover which was presented to each member of the Royal party who attended what was celebrated as the Centenary Year of the National.

King George VI and Queen Elizabeth were among a crowd of over 100,000 who applauded Evan Williams and Royal Mail, one of the few black horses to win the race and, although it was another nine years before Jim saw the National again, the great race had already made its mark on him. This was inevitable since his family had been associated with Aintree since 1839 – his great grandfather, Edward William Topham, was a member of the syndicate which staged the first National at Aintree in 1839.

Jim, who lives still in the splendid Paddock Lodge in the shadow of those oh, so ancient stands, is the nephew of the late, lamented Mirabel Topham, whose company Tophams Limited bought the racecourse from Lord Sefton in 1949. No one, surely, has been closer than Jim to the modern-day comings and goings surrounding the world's greatest steeplechase.

Jim was Mirabel's right-hand man and more than anyone knew just how much the great lady cared for Aintree and the National in particular. Aintree was under military occupation during the Second World War but no one was more keen than Mirabel to have the National back in full swing once the hostilities were over and she made an immediate visit to Downing Street to ensure that the troops were removed in time for the 1946 race. 'A great deal of damage had to be renovated within the stands,' recalled Jim, 'though the more serious problems concerned the course itself.

'Huge concrete blocks had been built in order to prevent planes landing on the wide, grassy expanse and these took a good deal of shifting. More particularly, the jumps themselves, which before the war were completely rebuilt every five years, were not able to be rebuilt in time and one of my vivid memories of the hurriedly-put-together 1946 race was the clouds of dust that blew out of some of

The thirty-three runners prepare to go to post in 1937, the year of Jim Bidwell-Topham's first visit to Aintree

the fences as the horses jumped through them.'

No one jumped better that year than Lovely Cottage, who had started at odds of 25–1 and was ridden by Captain Bobby Petre, an old school friend of Frank Furlong who had won the National eleven years earlier. Lovely Cottage had been sold to John Morant of Brockenhurst in Hampshire just four months before the race and was trained by Tommy Rayson near Winchester.

The National was very much back in business by the 1950s and Jim, as a Director and assistant Secretary, worked closely with Mirabel who was Chairman and Managing Director, and became increasingly identified with the big race.

It was a race which continued to provide thrills and spills and not a little controversy – take 1951 for example, memorable, sadly, for the number of fallers at the first fence, twelve out of thirty-six coming a cropper. Jim recalled: 'People may well have forgotten that in days gone by, sections of the National course were in fact ploughed fields; it was not all mown turf. The last relic of the plough, a small triangle between the Grand National start and the Melling Road, was used by our family to grow potatoes. It remained under plough right up to 1950 as

1935 – the water jump being dressed
for the big race

it was thought to steady the horses between the start and the first fence.

'However, the Stewards decided that it should be done away with, so we finished with the potatoes and the ground was duly turfed in time for the 1951 National. I can't help wondering whether that contributed to the almighty pile-up at the first fence.'

Jim enjoyed his administrative duties and responsibilities throughout the year at Aintree, helping his aunt with a multitude of things and being responsible for the total issue of complimentary badges – always a headache as any racecourse administrator will verify. He preferred to remain an anonymous figure behind the scenes on race days but in May 1956 his aunt persuaded him to succeed Major Peter Beckwith-Smith as Clerk of the Course, who was leaving for Hurst Park following the death of Sir John Crocker Bulteel, who himself had been a successful Clerk of the Course at Aintree.

Jim admits that he was reluctant to assume a role which many of his ancestors had filled with distinction but the Directors of Tophams – and Mirabel in particular – were keen to put his intimate knowledge of the operation to even greater use and Jim was at the helm as Fred Winter rode Sundew to victory in the

Mirabel Topham in the paddock of her beloved Aintree. 'The Grand National was her life'

1957 National, the first run on a Friday since 1944, though it reverted to a Saturday in 1958.

The Russians, who have only once entered horses in the National (1961), had caused something of a stir in 1956 when Georgi Malenkov, the former Russian Premier and his party, were privately entertained. They were guests of Mirabel for lunch and Jim recalled: 'They were accompanied by Mr Gromyko, the Russian Foreign Minister, who together with his wife and Mr Malenkov paraded themselves down the racecourse in front of the stands, thereby causing a good deal of comment in view of the fact that it was a strictly private visit. And all the time they were in the Topham's box, two Russian guards with pistols on their hips remained outside!'

Jim's main concern in the early days of his spell as Clerk of the Course was the effect of sponsored racing on the National. 'I was always worried that the National, as the greatest steeplechase in the world, should also remain the richest. The Company, however, could not afford to keep on increasing prize money each year and it was particularly pleasing when we had an invitation, fostered by my aunt, from Captain Spencer Freeman, the head of the Irish Hospital Trust, to stay with him in February 1958. The Trust agreed to sponsor the National and with their assistance and help from future sponsors such as British Petroleum, the National has remained ahead of any other chase.

'Our trip to Ireland in 1958 was made more enjoyable by Captain Freeman taking us on some wonderful tours of racing stables and I particularly recall one incident as we visited Tom Taaffe's yard. Mr What, who was entered for the National, was led out of his box and headed straight for my aunt who patted him on the nose and gave him a lump of sugar. The next day, an Irish paper reported the incident under the headline, "Mrs Topham's tip for the National." Mr What came over and won by thirty lengths from Tiberetta and I often wonder how many Irishmen followed that tip!'

The Tophams ran their last National in 1973 before the course was sold to Bill Davies of the Walton Group and they went out on an appropriate note as Jim explained . . .

'As far as my aunt and I were concerned, we could not have had a better winner in 1973 than Red Rum, who was owned by an old friend, Noel le Mare, who had been trying for years to win the National and, at the age of eighty-five, at last achieved his life's ambition.

'As it was the last race under Tophams, my aunt agreed to enter the unsaddling enclosure for the first and only time and present the solid gold trophy to Mr le Mare, who was so overcome by it all that he needed support as he staggered backwards. It was a delightful victory, one which gave us great pleasure.

'I am often asked about my aunt and can only say that over the years we had a very good business relationship. She was a wonderful person to work for, very fair and very straight; she would tell you off if you did wrong but praise you if you had done well. If we had disagreements, we always ironed them out. She listened to the other person's point of view and was a wonderful Chairman and Managing Director of the Company for forty years. The Grand National was her life.'

Peter Bromley

Peter Bromley, BBC racing correspondent since 1959, had them on their feet in the Hippodrome, Moscow, when he travelled behind the Iron Curtain with tales of the Grand National three weeks before the 1961 race which featured for the one and only time, horses from Russia.

Bromley's Russian connection provides a unique insight into an ill-conceived but enthusiastic assault on Aintree which was inspired by Moussia Soskin, a white Russian living in England at the time with trade connections in Moscow.

'Soskin encouraged the Russians to earmark three horses for the Grand National,' recalled Bromley, 'though it was with enthusiasm rather than professionalism, I'm afraid, for they were not sent over early enough to get handicapped. The three were good horses who had won big staying races but they were automatically given top weight of 12st which had the Russians up in arms because they didn't understand and thought they were being unfairly penalised.

'It was a venture full of sporting instincts but it would have been better if they had waited another year and sent the horses over in the autumn before the National.'

Strange that the Russians, normally so meticulous in getting the planning spot-on down to the very last detail, entered the National arena ill-prepared as Bromley discovered when he flew to Moscow with a BBC cameraman to film the horses in preparation. 'Mind you, how one could prepare a horse in ten degrees of frost on ice and snow was beyond one's belief. When the English jockeys heard I was going, they clubbed together and bought three English whips for me to present to the Russian jockeys.' The whips, made of whalebone, leather and silver inscribed 'Grand National 1961' were for show not for racing – and Bromley duly handed them over in the club room at the Hippodrome in Moscow where he showed a film of the previous year's National to an invited audience of enthusiasts, trainers and jockeys.

'I'd also taken maps of Aintree with me to help brief the jockeys and trainers and at the end of the film show, everyone stood up and cheered. It was the most

Peter Bromley en route to Moscow with the three whips bought by English jockeys to mark the 1961 debut of Russian entries in the National

marvellous thing they had ever seen. The first question I was asked afterwards was: could a horse fall, get up, be remounted and go on to win the race? Then they asked if the film had been speeded up! They had never seen anything like it.

'I returned to England convinced that they faced an impossible task. It was a forlorn hope really – and the travelling arrangements just about killed the whole thing. The horses had the most hair-raising 2,000-mile journey across Europe, going by train and then ship to Harwich, and on by train again to the north and Haydock Park where I had arranged for them to be stabled. I met them at Harwich and one horse, the best of the three in fact, Epigraph, was a very sick horse. They just about kept him alive.

'The Haydock Executive did everything to make them welcome and had made up several of the fences to look like National obstacles by facing them with gorse and the Russians were able to school over them.

'The other major problem to my mind was their reins which just weren't long enough for Aintree drop fences. They had the most dreadful Russian saddlery, the most grotty leather. I even got Bruce Hobbs, with the aid of a saddlery firm, to come up to Liverpool with a complete set of bridles and reins. The jockeys wanted to use them but the chief of the Russian party said, "Niet, we must use Russian saddles and bridles." You can only try to help – that was the sad part about the whole thing, if only they had asked for advice earlier . . .'

Come the National and only Reljef and Grifel were fit to run and, as Bromley feared, the saddlery brought about Grifel's downfall. 'His jockey, Prakhov, was pulled out of the saddle by the reins at Becher's first time. The horse lunged and wanted his head and poor Prakhov went straight out of the saddle.' Grifel was remounted but pulled up at the water while Reljef and Ponomarenko parted company at Valentine's.

The race, won by Nicolaus Silver, saw Bromley in the BBC radio commentary team for the first time and he has not missed a National for them since; he was, in fact, involved with television in 1960 and that particular race provides his most amusing National memory.

'BBC television, who were covering the National for the first time, had built the most enormous scaffolding down at the far end of the course near the Canal Turn. It was the biggest scaffolding I've ever had to work from, about eighty or ninety feet high; the cameraman was right on top, with me just below in the second tier. It gave me virtually an aerial view. I could see all the way up the first six fences but I had a bad view of Becher's where they dropped out of sight. Then they came round and went down past me.

'I'd told Ryan Price and Fred Winter about this and both their wives asked if they could come up with me and watch the race. I agreed, of course, and so all three of us climbed this terrible scaffolding which meant negotiating four pairs of ladders swaying in the wind!

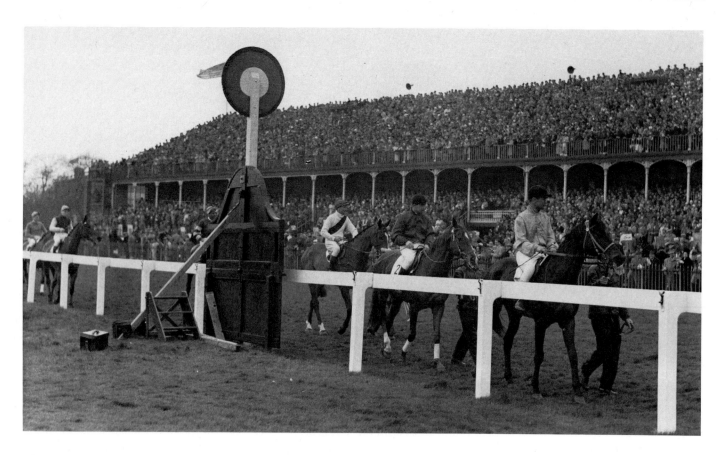

The Russians at Aintree – Reljef (1) and Grifel (2) lead the parade in 1961 with Merryman II (3), the previous year's winner, behind

'The inevitable happened – Fred Winter, who was on Dandy Scot, fell right below us at the Canal Turn. And while I was concentrating on the race, I was suddenly aware of this jockey in racing colours appearing at my side, tapping me on the shoulder and saying, "Watcha!" It was Fred, having climbed the tower "Mind if I watch from here?" he asked. I said, "No, so long as you get out of my way!" And there he stayed until the race was over when I took him back to the weighing-room in the car. As it was, I was grateful for his help in getting the girls back down the scaffolding; it really was hairy transferring from one ladder to another.'

Winter did not need Bromley's shoulder to lean on in 1962 when he stormed home on Kilmore for Ryan Price, who always gave a National Eve party in the Adelphi for the leading jockeys. 'Ryan went outside every hour to watch the rain pouring down,' said Bromley, 'and kept coming back and saying, "This is just what we want; the more rain the better." The four and a half miles on soft going caught everyone out but Kilmore that day, but Ryan's little horse just stayed and

Grifel comes to grief at Becher's: his jockey, Prakhov, was pulled out of the saddle by the reins when the horse lunged

stayed and beat Wyndburgh by ten lengths.'

Bromley, who enjoyed 'a short, sweet career' as a jump jockey until a fractured skull spoiled his dream – 'my ambition was to be the equivalent of Bryan Marshall as an amateur' – still thrills to the magic of the National after more than twenty years of calling them home.

'We've had some marvellous finishes. I would think Red Rum and Crisp was probably the most dramatic. It was the saddest thing to see Crisp beaten that day. If the race had been a few yards shorter, he'd surely have won. Then there was Red Rum's third National when the spectators came across the course and almost prevented him from finishing. He was galloping into a funnel at the end; there might have been another disaster like Devon Loch.

'And what about Bob Champion and Aldaniti. I doubt if there was a dry eye in the house. I didn't cope with the emotion that year. I readily admit that I blubbed like a baby. John Oaksey and I were in tears. I just about managed to keep my self-control before handing over to John to do a summary. The tears were pretty

1960 was the first televised National. The camera records the action as Tea Fiend leads from Badanloch, who finished second, with the eventual winner, Merryman II, behind them

real. It was so amazing, a fairy tale come true. It was exactly what everyone wanted to happen.

'I think the Derby is perhaps more important to me professionally in that I do the commentary on my own whereas I'm involved with three other commentators for the National. But I think the build-up, the excitement, the sensational stage and scenario of the Grand National course puts it in number one place.

'I really do feel quite frightened for the competitors when they are lining up before the race. I think that any moment now one of them could be coming back on a stretcher. That fear of danger, I suppose, is what lifts it out of the ordinary. Aintree is an amazing course, an astonishing arena for great events to happen. And great events do happen year after year. The National always comes up with something extraordinary that is talked about for the twelve months until the next one . . .'

David Coleman

When it comes to a question of sport and, more particularly, presenting or commentating on sport for television, then David Coleman has few peers: and when it comes to a question of the Grand National, then Coleman punctuates the air with that impassioned phrase that is his hallmark . . . 'To me, it's the best annual broadcast in any year.

'From a television point of view, it is extremely difficult and calls upon every discipline but I'm interested in National Hunt racing anyway. I know a lot of the people and those you have to deal with in National Hunt racing are probably the nicest people in sport. Taking it a stage further, it's an interesting fact that people who live in sport involved with danger are the most co-operative you find. Nothing is too much trouble and the National itself produces some marvellous stories and some of the most graphic interviews of all.'

The millions around the world who enjoy the National via BBC television would undoubtedly agree that David Coleman's post-race interviews with the winning jockey, trainer and owners which he has been doing since 1961 are certainly the most emotion-charged we see on our screens – Cliff Michelmore did the first in 1960 because illness forced Coleman to stay in London and he was not involved in the 1977 programme.

Coleman, who was a member of the Royal Commission on Gambling in the late seventies, has a remarkable feel for the big occasion and a particular passion for the National.

'I had always followed the National long before I was involved and it's always been a lucky race. My family like a bob or two on the horses and I've been backing the National winner ever since Royal Mail won at 100–6 in 1937. I generally back three or four horses and I've nearly always had the winner since I've been doing the race. I very much wanted Josh Gifford to win on Honey End in 1967 but he was second in that remarkable race to the 100–1 outsider, Foinavon. And guess which horse I drew in the BBC sweep – yes, Foinavon!' Maybe that's the secret of Coleman's winning smile as the successful jockey is thrust before the cameras to tell his story for the first time!

David Coleman, microphone in hand, prepares to interview the connections of Fred Rimell's second winner, Nicolaus Silver in 1961

Bobby Beasley was first into Coleman's hands after riding Nicolaus Silver to victory in 1961 and Fred Winter next in 1962 – 'That was marvellous. I knew Fred well from working in the Midlands and his twins are roughly the same age as mine, David and Dean. I'd long admired Kilmore's trainer, Ryan Price, a real character, and the owner Nat Cohen made good interviewing, too, so they were all good value.

'But the following year's National threw up a remarkable story. John Oaksey "rode" the National course for the BBC in a helicopter, the first time that it had ever been done. He did this several days before the National and described the thrill of jumping the last fence and being in the race with a chance, how he would feel coming up the run-in. When it came to the race itself, you could fit John's commentary alongside the actuality as he so nearly won on Carrickbeg. He had written the script for that race; it was remarkable.

'There was something else quite remarkable about the 1963 National. During the week I had a letter from Teasy Weasy's publicity agent saying he would be coming up to the National and I should be sure to interview him before the race because he had something fascinating to say. Of course, I didn't take any notice of it but on the Friday evening, the telephone rang in my hotel and my wife Barbara answered it – she always does my background work at Aintree which she loves – and it was this publicity agent again. She said I was making a big mistake not interviewing Teasy Weasy and though I told her there was not a hope in hell as we were full, she said he would come to see me just before two o'clock. But he didn't turn up and I forgot all about it until his horse, Ayala, won the race!

'Teasy Weasy was in the winner's enclosure again in 1976 after Rag Trade's victory had given Fred Rimell his record-breaking fourth National – and I couldn't stop him! Something had happened elsewhere and we were madly trying to go over to another event when he suddenly burst into song. I remember someone saying, "We start out with the Grand National and end up with the Eurovision Song Contest!"'

In recent years, there has been an almost paranoid desire by jockeys to be interviewed before the race. 'I think I'm right in saying,' said Coleman, 'that apart from Johnny Buckingham, the National has always been won by a jockey who was interviewed by the BBC beforehand, during the time we take a look at the course with the riders. Certainly, we interview ten to a dozen but remember that there have never been fewer than twenty-six runners since we started in 1960 and there have been over forty on eight occasions.'

Coleman is swift to praise everyone in the BBC team – over two-hundred are at Aintree. Twenty miles of cable are laid down and twenty cameras are used, compared with four at a football match, for example. 'The National is a tremendous tribute to the BBC engineers. It is one of the biggest tasks they undertake because it covers so much ground. The boys take a special pride in making sure it's right and we've had very few technical problems over the years.

'Certainly, it's a difficult programme to do because you're out on a limb linking everything from the site. We don't have a script, it's all ad lib but the technical side is fantastic and the facilities the boys lay on give me a comparatively easy ride. It's a pleasure to do the National.'

Nowadays, Coleman joins the riggers in the Control Room to watch the race. 'I tried to watch from the Press Stand but it was impossible. There's just not enough information there, you don't know what's happening on the far side. I get the complete story from the Control Room and as soon as they've passed the post, I belt across to the winner's enclosure to meet the winning connections.'

And those interviews are the moments many treasure more than anything – not least Coleman himself. 'There have been so many personal associations with the winners over the years that, naturally, it has made the interviews even more enjoyable.

'Willie Robinson, for example, who won on Team Spirit in 1964. I knew him very well and we stayed in the Adelphi as he did. Tommy Smith, the following year. What a marvellous story! We followed Fred Winter when he walked the course with Tommy beforehand, telling him where to go. If you remember, Tommy might have drawn a line around the course, he followed Fred's pattern everywhere. It was really remarkable.

Bob Champion talks David Coleman through the 1981 race. 'There was tremendous emotion in the unsaddling area after Aldaniti's win,' recalled Coleman

'Then Tim Norman, who won again for Fred in 1966 on the 50–1 outsider Anglo. He was absolutely thrilled to bits. I remember going with him to the American Sporting Club where I was the guest speaker on the Monday afterwards and he was suddenly promoted to Guest of Honour. Tim never had it so good before or since.

'Eddie Harty in 1969 gave me one of the most graphic after-race interviews ever following his win on Highland Wedding. Eddie's a great mate of mine for all sorts of reasons, from horse dealing to talking! Two years later, Eddie and Terry Biddlecombe came down at the first. I remember talking to them afterwards off the air, and they were going berserk. After falling, they'd been going up and down the Melling Road cursing. I then actually interviewed them for television at about twenty to five and they were hilarious by that stage. They'd got over their initial disappointment although I don't think Biddlecombe would really ever get over it because he'd missed the winning ride on Gay Trip in 1970 because of injury and was in fact on Gay Trip in '71 and they were the 8–1 favourites. Then he was second on him the following year.

'Fred Pontin is another good friend who ended up in the winner's enclosure after his horse Specify won in 1971. Barbara and I had dinner with Fred and his trainer, the late John Sutcliffe, the night before, so that was another winner I backed!'

Coleman's most frequent interviewees, of course, have been Red Rum's trainer, Ginger McCain and owner, Noel le Mare. 'What a marvellous old man Mr le Mare was and, of course, in 1973 he came out with those now immortal lines, "I have had three aims ever since I was a young man: to marry a beautiful girl, to become a millionaire and to win the Grand National. Now I have achieved them all and it has made my life."

'Without doubt, Raymond Guest, the American owner of L'Escargot, was one of the most emotional winners of all. He was at the next table to me having a private dinner party the previous night at the Adelphi and was completely charged up. They really fancied the horse though he had failed in three previous attempts. Raymond was literally trembling when I interviewed him after the race; when I put the mike towards him after asking a question, he grabbed it and I couldn't get the thing out of his hand.'

Coleman chuckled at the memory of one after-race scenario. 'The winning owner staggered through the crowds into the unsaddling enclosure and by the time he arrived looked very pale and shaken. I asked if he was all right and he said, "Leave me alone for a minute, then I'll be fine." He was joined a moment later by a lady wearing an Ascot-type outfit completely wrong for Aintree who asked me: "May I be interviewed?" I asked if she was the owner's wife? She said, "No, I'm his friend!" I don't know what that was all about . . .'

Coleman has enjoyed every one of those interviews but picks Aldaniti's

Charlie Fenwick tells David Coleman the story of Ben Nevis's victory in 1980

triumph as his happiest memory. 'I knew the whole scene very well for we have been friends of Josh Gifford's wife Althea for many years. We had Havana Royal from her family, the Roger-Smiths, and my daughter Anne, who is now married to international show-jumper Tony Newbery, won the British champion-ship on that horse.

'There was tremendous emotion in the unsaddling area after Aldaniti's win. Josh was practically in tears, the owners were practically in tears and Althea was in tears. The coolest character of all was Bob Champion, really.

'What a round Aldaniti's was in terms of pure jumping. It rivalled Crisp in 1973, not as spectacular maybe, but superb nonetheless. It gives me real pleasure to look at that tape and see Aldaniti jumping. Even now, some people still talk about the National being cruel but I don't think it is. Look at the way those horses jump the fences, they really enjoy it.'

Coleman admits that if he had not become so involved in the world of show jumping – he is a director of Hickstead – then he would have liked to own

National Hunt horses and, who knows, even a Grand National runner or two.

No matter, he follows the jumping game keenly and leaves you in no doubt about his feelings for Aintree and the National in particular. 'It is nonsense for people to talk about Liverpool being unable to support racing. Maybe there wasn't a public for the sort of racing they used to stage at Aintree but Ladbrokes have shown, with their organisation and John Hughes's stage management, that there is a market in Liverpool. The race has more public impact than any single annual sporting event. It's just a question of spectacle and there's nothing to compare with the National.'

Ossie Dale

The Grand National means many things to many people all over the world but to Ossie Dale it means quite simply – 'My whole life.' Nothing more, nothing less since the summer of 1953 when Mirabel Topham first took him on the groundstaff to drive the shire horses for the farm in the centre of the course.

By the National meeting of 1954, Ossie had become stable manager and begun to eat, sleep and drink the world's greatest steeplechase until it became his staple diet. He turned his office by the entrance to Paddock Yard into a shrine to the National, filling it with pictures and souvenirs – home from home for this engaging Evertonian, who was brought up in Diana Street opposite Goodison Park and whose first memories of the National go back to Jump Sunday.

'A pal and I played truant from Sunday School every year to join in the fun of Jump Sunday. I loved it – the tipsters, the merry-go-rounds, the noise, the colour, it was smashing. My mother would give me two-pence for the collection and I'd spend it on a penny tram-ride to Aintree and back. I often wondered why she never twigged, for it was the only Sunday of the year that I never complained about going to Sunday school!'

The Sunday before the National took on a whole new meaning for Ossie once he took charge of the stables, for each year he packed his bags and left his wife, Joan, at home in Lydiate, a bike-ride from the course, to move into Aintree. He converted a room above his cosy office into a bedroom fit for a week and settled down to look after the horses.

In those early years, the Irish horses arrived as early as Tuesday and Ossie's earthy smile was always there to greet the lads and lasses from the Emerald Isle. Perhaps that is why he has formed a special affection for the Irish. 'They turned up with a great trunk full of medicines and goodness knows what for the horses,' said Ossie, 'and I always pulled their legs by insisting on searching the trunk thoroughly for bombs!'

And it is an Irish-trained horse, L'Escargot, which provided Ossie with his greatest National memory – and souvenir. He was given one of the shoes worn by Dan Moore's brilliant chestnut gelding in 1975 and Ossie had it mounted on a

Ossie Dale puts his feet up in his office by the entrance to Paddock Yard, a shrine to the National. He is holding a shoe worn by L'Escargot in 1975 that he had mounted, and a champagne-bottle reminder of the celebrations after that victory

plaque which occupies a special place in the shrine in the stable block.

'L'Escargot was one of the horses to arrive on the Tuesday before the race,' recalled Ossie, 'and it was always a delight to see him. He'd fallen the first year he ran in the National but I put him in No. 1 box right next door to me in 1973 and he finished third. He was back there the following year and finished second to Red Rum. I felt sure it would be third time lucky in 1975 – and it was!

'I sat and chatted with Mick Ennis, Dan Moore's head lad, on the Thursday morning along with Jack Kidd, who was Fred Rimell's travelling head lad. "What's L'Escargot going to do this time?" I asked Mick. He put on his best Michael O'Hehir voice and said, "If he's standing at Becher's second time round, he'll win." I said to Mick, "Are you sure about that?" and he said, "Sure, I'm sure, and I'll tell you another thing, Red Rum will be second." Amazing, that's just the way they finished.

'L'Escargot was one of the real class horses to contest the National, of course, but more than that, to me, he was a lovely bedside companion! A perfect horse, no trouble at all, so quiet. I never had any worry about going into his box. He was a real Christian, as the Irish would say. We had a wonderful evening after that National. Mick Ennis popped his head into my office and said, "I've had a word with Mr Guest [Raymond Guest, the owner of L'Escargot], and I've asked him to send over a crate of champagne to the stables." Sure enough, he did. Well, I was floating on air.'

Ossie took home an empty champagne bottle on the Sunday evening and later had a picture of L'Escargot in the stables stuck on the bottle – another happy entry in his diary. The Grand National book which the late Clive Graham and Bill Curling wrote is one more of Ossie's treasures, and is unique for he invites every winning jockey and trainer to sign the book – 'There are some wonderful names in there, bringing back some wonderful memories.'

Ossie counts the late Fred Rimell among the best pals he made along the National way; maybe because all four of Rimell's record-breaking winners were stabled with Ossie in Paddock Yard – Gay Trip and Rag Trade each occupying the same box, in fact. 'Once a trainer has won the National, he likes to have the same box in following years,' said Ossie, who makes a name plate to put over the door of the stable each winning horse occupies.

'ESB in 1956 was my first winner in Paddock Yard and I was very excited because, with only thirty-nine boxes as against 137 in the New Yard, my chances of housing the winner was naturally much smaller. I like to think, too, that I played my own small part in ESB's victory. He had to be given some medication a few hours before a race to prevent his bursting blood vessels and Jack Kidd called me over at midnight before the race to ask me to give a helping hand. I can remember holding ESB's head up in the air so Jack could pour the stuff down his throat!'

And twenty-six years later, before the 1982 National, Ossie turned vet to help one of the fancied horses whose trainer had forgotten to administer a vitamin injection which was due on the Monday before the race. 'He'd been up to the yard in the morning but had forgotten to give the injection and the horse's lass came to me and asked if I could do it. She said she couldn't possibly stick a needle in the horse. "Good heavens, it wouldn't bother me," I said, "but I wouldn't know if I was doing it right." She told me it was simple enough, so I agreed to do it; I banged his muscle on the chest and in went the needle!'

You name it, Ossie's seen it if it has anything to do with the National – and he's seen some things which have nothing to do with it at all. 'I'll never forget the night an English girl who was with one of the Irish stables came with one of the other lads after midnight and knocked on my door asking to see their horse. Now that's quite normal, of course, on the night before the National; the lad often wants to

Top: Ossie Dale marks the box that Well To Do and Ben Nevis occupied before their victories

Below: Tea Fiend and Gerry Maddon show how to clear the water jump as they lead the 1960 field – unlike the racegoer whom Ossie Dale watched land in the water as he attempted to jump it for his children!

check and make sure all is well. I gave them the key with some misgivings because they'd obviously had a drink or two. Well, I waited and waited for them to return the key; in the end, I went over to the box which was in the far corner of the yard and opened the door very quietly. I don't know what the horse thought, but there they were, the young couple, in the middle of a love-making session! I closed the door gently and crept halfway back across the yard and then shouted, "Are you coming, I'm waiting to go to bed?" The reply was, "Yes!"'

One incident above all others really brings tears to Ossie's eyes. It goes back to a National morning in the sixties when he was walking the course with Steve Westhead, the racecourse foreman until his death in 1980. 'Coming along in the opposite direction between The Chair and the water jump was a chap all dressed to kill with his wife and a couple of youngsters. The water jump in those days really was a water jump, with water three feet deep at one end and about a foot deep at the shallow end. But the fence itself is one of the smallest on the course. The kids pointed to the water jump and shouted, "Daddy, you could jump that." He said, "Yes, I could." And with that, took a running jump, landing in the water up to his waist! I've never seen such a startled look on anyone's face. The tears of laughter were streaming down my face.'

That man and his deflated ego was all Ossie had ever seen jump his beloved Aintree fences until the 1981 National, his first as the racecourse foreman. 'I never once saw the race before Aldaniti's win; I always stayed in Paddock Yard and waited for the race to finish, then I'd run to the gate and count the horses as they came in. I was never happy unless all those who went out came back.'

Alas, over the years, a number of horses have not come back and that is the one tinge of sadness which clouds Ossie's National memories. 'You see, I love the horses,' he said, 'and I really do get butterflies in my stomach each year before the National. Butterflies for the horses. After all, we've been sleeping together for many years . . .'

Reg Green

You won't find the name Reg Green on the Grand National Roll of Honour, nor even among the also-rans but if there is anything you want to know about the world's greatest steeplechase, then Reg Green is your man. An Evertonian, born in 1937, he has devoted every spare minute of his life to unearthing anything and everything about the National until his delightful detached house in Aughton near Ormskirk – barely a couple of Grand National circuits away from the course – houses surely one of the finest collections of National memorabilia.

Every book that has ever been written about the National is there; a pictorial record of every race since the turn of the century; National racecards covering several decades plus newspaper cuttings to fill a Fleet Street library.

'I'm something of a freak if you like,' said Reg, and his wife Brenda would not

Reg Green at home with some of his National mementoes

Mrs Partridge brings in her horse, Sprig, and Ted Leader after the 1927 National – one of Reg Green's early memories

disagree for she has lived with his obsession for the National since 26 March 1960 – their wedding day and, yes, Grand National Day! Even his wedding could not keep him from the race which he has missed live just once since 1946, that was when Brenda was in hospital in 1982 – 'Then I sat on the edge of her bed and watched it on the tele,' said Reg almost apologetically.

Reg's love affair began during the Second World War when he went with his father to Aintree for the first time. 'I was about six and was enraptured by Dad's stories of the National. Father had lost quite a bit of money on the horses and didn't back at all for two years. Then, in 1927, he staked everything on Sprig and it won at 8–1. I remember being quite transfixed as Dad told the story of Sprig. How his owner, Mrs Partridge who was seventy-four at the time, had bred Sprig and kept him in training as a memorial really for her son who had been killed shortly before the Armistice.

'It was all too much for me to take in at the time for Aintree was littered with American armoured vehicles as the Yanks had taken it over during the war. I don't know whether it was the way Dad told the story or what, but the words "Grand National" seemed magical and I determined then, even at that age, to

In 1937, the winning post gets a coat
of paint before the big day – from
Reg Green's collection of unusual
pictures connected with the National

find out everything I could about this great race and see it when it started again.'
Reg was there alongside his father when the National was next run in 1946 – 'And
it was just as I had imagined, except more so. It was wonderful.'

Reg was hooked and from then on it was the same routine every Sunday; a
tram from Everton to Aintree to soak up its atmosphere. 'I soon found a way in to
the course at Anchor Bridge and I'd sit in the well at Becher's and dream of what
I'd read.'

The boy became a teenager and the teenager became a man but the routine on
Sunday was alway the same. 'I just never tired of the place. I was never a great one
for history at school but to me the National had the aura of the Charge of the
Light Brigade as the horses raced across the Melling Road and out into the
country. I'd be on my own for fifty-one Sundays of the year, but Jump Sunday
was different – that was carnival time as the place began to come alive in
readiness for the National.'

As Reg's knowledge of the race grew – no one has yet asked him a question he
could not answer – so his obsession for its preservation grew, too, and in 1975 he
drew up plans to form a Grand National Supporters' Association. 'The race once
more looked in real trouble and I desperately wanted to do something to help,' he
said. 'Sadly, I could never get the idea off the ground though I had leaflets printed
and talks with the owners of the course, the local council and prominent people in
racing. All I wanted was to help preserve the race so I could take my
grandchildren to see it in years to come. It hurt me deeply when I was challenged:
"What do *you* want out of it, pal?"'

But nothing has – or could it seems – dimmed Reg's enthusiasm for the race, and certainly not his inability to pick the winner. 'I even failed on my wedding day and I couldn't have had a better tip,' he said.

'There was a huge hotel, the Imperial, opposite Lime Street Station in those days, which included a real old-fashioned barber's shop, about thirty chairs and an equal number of barbers all in line. I decided to treat myself to the works, a facial, the lot. After all, it was my Wedding Day . . . and Grand National Day!

'All I could see of the fella in the chair next to me was a pair of jodphurs and riding boots for he was lying flat and fully towelled. My ears pricked up as the man's conversation with the barber turned to racing. We were more or less finished at the same time and when the fella got up I recognised him as Gerry Scott, the jockey. I had my National souvenir edition of the local paper with me and asked Gerry to autograph it, asking him, "What's going to win today?" "Well," he said, "you could do a lot worse than back my fella." His horse was Merryman II, who had won the Foxhunters the previous year.

'Off I went to my wedding thrilled to bits. We had a quick reception in the centre of Liverpool and my best man had organised a taxi to take us straight to the course. We arrived a bit late, just as they were lining up so I forgot all about having a bet and, of course, Gerry Scott and Merryman II drew away to win unchallenged. I've backed plenty of seconds in the National but *never* the winner!'

But there is more, much, much more to the National than trying to find the winner as far as Reg is concerned. 'To my mind, all the horses and jockeys deserve a mention every year just for taking part,' he said, flicking through another album and reeling off the names of every jockey and every horse in every picture he possesses.

He spent £300 shortly after being married – 'Brenda insisted that we beg, borrow the money somehow' – on a collection of National books and photographs to augment his own and now his Sunday routine after every National is the same. 'I buy every paper and select the pictures I want, then write off for copies. When I began, the photographs were only one shilling each, now they are nearer one pound.'

It is not unusual for local clubs and associations to invite him to give a talk on the National – 'And that's where my photographs are a real bonus. Some of the tales need some believing but people are amazed when they see the photographs. It is nice, for example, to be able to show that Tipperary Tim really did finish alone in 1928 – Billy Barton was remounted to finish second – from the then largest field of all, forty-two. The conditions were altered the following year to try to reduce the number of runners; it had the opposite effect and a record sixty-six went to post and I show them actually having to line up in two rows. Surprisingly, not one fell at the first that year and Easter Hero, who had caused

all the trouble in 1928, ran the race of his life to finish second to Gregalach.'

What is his greatest National memory? 'They're all wonderful, but I've never seen a finish like 1954 when Royal Tan and Bryan Marshall held off Tudor Line and George Slack by a neck. And Red Rum's third victory, well, that was something really special, just as Aldaniti's triumph was in 1981 . . . but they're all wonderful.'

Reg Green no longer spends every Sunday sitting in the well of Becher's – 'But I have to admit that I make a point of passing the course every day if possible and I always go over Anchor Bridge and along the Melling Road dreaming my dreams as I go.'

Above: Tipperary Tim finishes alone in 1928 with the riderless Great Span

Left: 1955, the only time the water jump has been omitted from the National, because of water on the course

Michael O'Hehir

If imitation is the greatest form of flattery, then Michael O'Hehir, the friendly little wizard of Irish racing, has made it big. For each year, Aintree is suddenly taken over by hundreds of would-be Mike Yarwoods when O'Hehir's BBC radio commentary on the Grand National is switched into the course circuit and broadcast over the public address system.

People in the enclosures and stands, on the buses and the banks, 'do their Michael O'Hehir' as he calls the race from his perch at Becher's. Perhaps not everyone knows the face behind the Voice but O'Hehir's voice is as 'Aintree' as Becher's to millions around the world for whom O'Hehir is their window on the National. The Voice has been missing for only two years since 1946 – first in 1947, when the BBC North of England, as they were then, decided to handle the race and left O'Hehir out of their team and then, in 1952, when Aintree owner Mirabel Topham organised her own commentary team.

'On three occasions, she sent a representative over to Ireland to find out whether I would head up her team,' recalled O'Hehir. 'She offered £500, a lot of money at the time, which put me in a spot. I didn't know quite what to do. I had always worked freelance for the BBC so there was nothing actually to prevent me from taking on the task but I decided that I would stick with my BBC colleagues; on balance, I'm glad I didn't take up the offer, although I would have hoped to have made some improvement on the dismal performance organised by Mrs Topham. That was one of her greatest disasters and the following year, the broadcast reverted into the safe hands of the BBC, who had broadcast every previous race since 1927.'

Mrs Topham's broadcast was unbelievable. Mr Kirkpatrick, her principal gateman, found himself at the microphone with a ten-minute spot to fill because of a delay to the start and then Teal, the eventual winner, was wrongly announced as a first fence faller! The commentator at Becher's – O'Hehir's regular spot – could stutter no more than 'Up and over' without mentioning even one horse by name.

O'Hehir, an acknowledged authority, incidentally, on Gaelic football and

Tic-tac men at Aintree, 1957-style

hurling, still played a part in the 1947 broadcast of the race which he watched from the stands overlooking the finish. 'I've seen every race bar 1947 from Becher's since my first broadcast in 1946 and I wouldn't have a clue what it's like to watch from the stands though nowadays the television monitor enables me to enjoy the finish.'

The 1947 race was run in dreadful conditions – pouring rain, hock-deep mud and poor visibility. 'I was there standing by Raymond Glendenning who had the unenviable task of trying to broadcast in the fog. Caughoo, a 100–1 shot owned by a Dublin jeweller, Jack McDowell, and trained by his veterinary surgeon brother Herbie, and Lough Conn came out of the fog towards the finish a long way in front of the rest.

'Claude Harrison, Raymond's race reader, spotted Lough Conn all right but neither of them could identify the other horse. I was pretty sure it was Caughoo

Caughoo, the 100–1 outsider, is led
in after winning in 1947

by the time they approached the second last fence but neither Raymond nor
Claude had yet got him and even when they jumped the last more or less together,
it was still a one-horse commentary. I had twice shouted, "It's Caughoo," but it
wasn't until halfway up the run-in that Raymond, in desperation, said, "Michael
O'Hehir, who should know something about the Irish, tells me it's Caughoo."
He was adequately covering himself!

'It certainly was Caughoo, who won easily in the end – a great victory for the
McDowell family who had bought Caughoo for fifty guineas as an unbroken
two-year-old. They had even debated beforehand whether to go for the Ulster
National instead of Aintree. They certainly made the right decision.'

O'Hehir, the first racecourse commentator in Britain and Ireland, has been
associated with American television coverage of the world's major races but he
has no doubt where he places the Grand National. 'It's the greatest race on earth.
If I could only see one race a year, I would choose the National every time.'

He has a host of Aintree memories since he went, with his father, to see his first
National in 1939. It was won by Workman and the emotion and drama of this
unique race left a lasting impression on him. O'Hehir has no doubt, however,
about his greatest National memory – it concerns the 1967 race won by Foinavon,
the fourth horse to win at odds of 100–1 in the history of the National.

'I was standing in the weighing-room checking out the colours as I always do.
There was a long line of jockeys and in the middle was this jockey with a black
jacket and red and yellow braces that threw me completely. Now, I'd done my
homework on the horses and had my little cards with all the colours crayoned on
them and I flicked through them, looked down the racecard and no way could I
see anything like black with red and yellow braces. "What the hell's this?" I
thought and went over to the jockey who was Johnny Buckingham. His mount
was completely unconsidered and nobody had given it a moment's thought so the
name of the horse certainly didn't come immediately to mind. "What's this?" I
asked, indicating his colours. When Johnny replied that it was Foinavon, I said,
"But when the horse ran at Cheltenham, he carried light green and dark green
quarters." "Oh, yes," said Johnny, "but the owner thought green was unlucky
and that he'd try these colours today for the first time."

'Without that chat, I'd have been completely lost when the drama unfolded
around me after Becher's second time around. There were still twenty-five or so
standing but after clearing Becher's and going on to the 23rd, two horses
suddenly went right across another and another and another, running up and
down the fence. There were fallers everywhere, I've never seen anything like it at
all. Not one horse could get over.

'Then all of a sudden, I looked back towards Becher's and there was the black
jacket with red and yellow braces – Foinavon, virtually tailed off. He was just
jumping Becher's! Now if I hadn't been lucky enough to have been standing

Tic-tac men at Aintree, 1982-style

where I was in the weighing-room, I'd have been scratching my head and wondering what the hell to say – wouldn't I have been in a mess!

'I was able to call Foinavon and Johnny Buckingham as they threaded their way through the chaos, up and over that fateful 23rd, and on over the final seven fences virtually alone to win in the end from Honey End and Josh Gifford, one of the eighteen from the original field of forty-four to eventually complete. But only Foinavon had cleared the 23rd at the first attempt.

'I knew Foinavon in Ireland when he was owned by Anne, Duchess of Westminster. He wasn't worth two shillings and was sold as a nothing. But that's one of the magical things about the National – anything can happen.

'When it comes to my more sentimental memories of the National, I think of Pat Taaffe. Not only did I admire him as a jockey, but he's been one of my best friends for years and is godfather to my son, Michael. When he first went over to Aintree, before he started riding heaps of winners, we used to share a room together in the Adelphi and the lack of tension in the man always amazed me. He might have been going out to ride hurdle races rather than the National. He was, of course, a natural horseman who grew up in the world of hunting and showing before progressing, via point-to-points, to steeplechasing. It always gave me a kick to see him do well and I was delighted by his two victories in the National – on Vincent O'Brien's third winner, Quare Times, and Fred Rimell's third winner, Gay Trip, a horse he originally recommended to Fred.'

The world's greatest steeplechase readily identifies with O'Hehir's voice and Aintree would never seem quite the same without his million-miles-an-hour delivery booming out across the track. And the race certainly wouldn't be the same for all those Mike Yarwoods!

Duque de Alburquerque

A film of a Grand National in the 1920s was the start of an amazing Aintree adventure for the Spaniard who found it among his presents on his eighth birthday in 1926. 'I had loved horses since a child. Now I saw this beautiful race, the greatest test of a horse and rider in the world. I said then I would win that race one day.'

Alas, the Duque de Alburquerque, a Spanish nobleman with a lineage that goes back to 1464, never did win the National though his courage – some say it was madness – earned him a fondly indulgent following among Aintree's afficionados.

The memories though are painful ones. It was 1952 before the Duque finally went to post in the National, on his own horse Brown Jack III who was trained for him by the late Peter Cazalet. The Duque had won on Brown Jack III at Lingfield a fortnight before Aintree and he already had one hardened admirer, the fearless Joe Sunlight who, at the time, had seen thirty Nationals and backed fifteen winners. Joe supported the Duque to win £10,000! The Duque and Brown Jack III crashed at the sixth fence. 'Poor animal, it was past it,' smiled the Duque. Poor animal, poor Duque! He woke up in hospital with a cracked vertebra, enough to put most men off for life.

The Duque returned to his estate outside Madrid, got himself fit and well again and rode the racetracks of Europe, never forgetting for one moment Aintree and the National. Ten years after his debut, he bought a twelve-year-old Irish horse Jonjo, who had started favourite for the 1961 National and finished seventh behind Nicolaus Silver. The horse rapped a tendon and had to miss the 1962 race but the Duque and Jonjo made it in 1963 – at least as far as the 21st where they fell and our hero collected some more bruises.

He bought another Irish-trained horse, Groomsman, to ride in the 1965 National. They fell at the 9th and the Duque went off to hospital with a broken leg, the twenty-second fracture of his life.

The following year was a very good year for the Duque and he went as far as the 26th before pulling up on L'Empereur; but it was 1973 and another ten

It's an upside-down world for Bobby Morrow as he parts company with Whispering Steel in 1952; the Duque de Alburquerque on Brown Jack III tracks Freebooter and Bryan Marshall

fractures later, before the Duque tried the National again. He rode the seven-year-old Nereo – the oldest rider and youngest horse – but fate dealt yet another cruel blow. 'A leather broke for the only time in my life. I kept on for eight more fences before pulling up before the Canal Turn. I could not give up trying then. It was so often like that. Every year provided the excuse to try just once more.'

By then the Duque's obsession with the National had become a Very Important Part of the race and the bookmakers, ever happy to oblige, began offering an amusing 66–1 against the Duque completing the course. In 1974, you were entitled to expect 500–1 against him even taking part.

The Duque, fifty-six-years-old at the time, had sixteen screws taken out of a leg – the result of an accident in Seville – two weeks before the National and the stitches were still raw on the day of the race. Worse still, he broke his collar-bone the week before! That was, however, his finest hour. His happiest memory . . .

The smile on the face of this stunningly impressive man said it all as he crossed the line on Nereo in eighth place. Seventeen of the forty-two starters completed

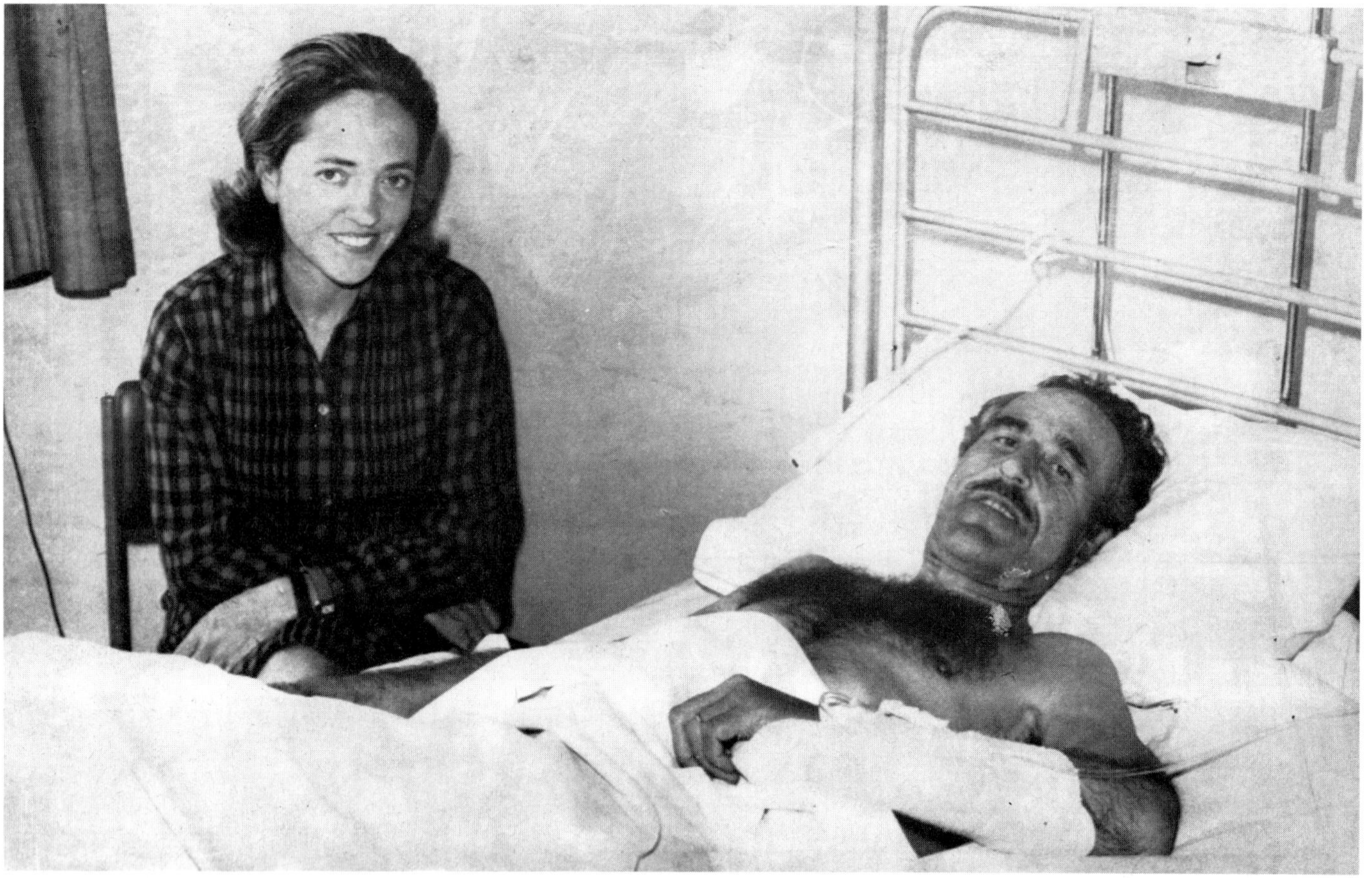

Above: 1976, Walton Hospital, so often the finishing post for the Duque de Alburquerque. His wife sits beside his bed after his horrific accident

the course as Red Rum won for the second successive year. The Duque dismounted defiant as ever. 'I sat like a sack of potatoes and gave the horse no help. It deserved another chance.'

They were all set to go, too, in 1975 but a week before the National, the Duque was hurled into a rail at Newbury and broke another leg. Even then he toyed with the idea of riding – until Fred Winter, who trained Nereo for him, reminded the Duque that it would be unfair to the horse. 'I have often been afraid on a horse,' observed the Duque, 'but fear is like any other habit, you learn to live with it. If a horse crashes, you may break a bone. If a car crashes, you may die. Do you then stop driving?'

The Duque, almost inevitably, came to the end of the National road on 3 April 1976, painfully, horrifically, frighteningly . . . once more, he was on the faithful Nereo. Once more, he was up with the leaders when he took the most dreadful fall at the 13th. 'I have been superstitious of the number 13 all my life.'

1974 was a vintage year for the Spanish nobleman. He finished eighth on Nereo, despite having broken his collar-bone a week before the race!

The Duque de Alberquerque and Jonjo, his partner until the twenty-first in the 1963 National

A stampede of hooves and loose horses passed over the Duque; nothing could prevent him being knocked about like a football. It was more than two days before he regained consciousness in the intensive care unit of Walton General Hospital, the finishing post for so many broken National dreams. The injury list was sickening even by the Duque's standards ... seven broken ribs, broken vertebrae, broken wrist, fractured right thigh bone, severe concussion.

Yet still he refused to quit. 'I still wanted to return and complete the course on a Spanish horse, though I admit that my chances of winning seemed remote then, but I do not regard age as something which automatically eliminates a man from doing anything.'

The Jockey Club, mercifully, refused the Duque permission to ride over fences or hurdles in Britain in 1977. For the first time, they had introduced a rule which required any amateur rider over fifty, whatever his nationality, to undergo medical examination. The Rule Book, not the most feared fences in steeplechasing, had finally beaten the Duque. 'I was very sad. I trained hard for the 1977 National and considered myself fitter than I had been for years and certainly in much better shape than when I finished eighth on Nereo in 1974 when I rode with a fractured collar-bone. Two months before the National I found it almost impossible to do up my shoe-laces and on many occasions I cried with pain during exercises I forced myself to do. But I did them and got back into form. Then they banned me.'

The Duque took his place in a private box and watched the 1977 National with Fred Winter – 'the saddest National of my life'. Robert Kington rode Nereo that day and they were close up when they fell second time round at Becher's; the following year, Nereo, ridden this time by Mark Floyd, made it all the way round again, fourteenth of the fifteen finishers from a field of thirty-seven.

The Duque has not been back to the National since but he leaves behind a multitude of memories, a brave and gallant sportsman.

Charlotte Brew

Charlotte Brew knew exactly what she wanted to do when she grew up – she wanted to ride in the Grand National, just as Elizabeth Taylor had. Difference was, Elizabeth Taylor's journey round Aintree was a celluloid caper for the movies called *National Velvet*; Charlotte, bless her heart, wanted to do the real thing.

So whenever the little girl from Coggeshall in Essex was given one wish the answer was always the same. 'I want to ride in the Grand National.' And the reaction of her parents, Judith and Richard, and their family was always the same: 'Poor little thing, she doesn't understand that women can't ride in the National.'

Charlotte began messing about with horses from the age of four, graduating to point-to-point races as a teenager and driving her parents potty with her obsession about the National. Every year, they sat in front of the television on National Day, had a bet – and Charlotte dreamed her dreams.

School days at Benenden revolved around horses for Charlotte – 'My parents persuaded the headmistress to let me ride twice a week and I was always getting into trouble for going to the stables when I wasn't meant to' – and when she finished there at eighteen, her parents agreed she could have a year off before going to Warwick University – 'to get this horse thing out of your system'.

She never did get horses out of her system and two years later, on Thursday 1 April 1976, the racing world and his wife knew all about the blonde with laughing green eyes and rings on her fingers, as she became the first woman to ride over the Aintree fences in the Greenall Whitley Foxhunters Chase. Fourth place behind Credit Call after safely negotiating the National fences for $2\frac{3}{4}$ miles meant that Charlotte's horse, Barony Fort, was qualified for the National itself; now she could have her wish. And on Saturday 2 April 1977, the twenty-one-year-old Charlotte Brew became the first woman to ride in the Grand National; what mayhem there was, what pandemonium.

'Looking back, I'd give the whole thing up tomorrow if it meant going through the pressures I had before the race,' recalled Charlotte. 'I had never imagined for one minute that things would turn out as they did. I'd had to fight hard with my parents during the summer of 1976 to persuade them to let me ride; it was one thing smiling sweetly when I wished my wish as a child and quite another facing up to the reality of it all. Then once they agreed and it became public, I felt like an object of curiosity, and life was pretty unbearable.

'I'd get up at six-thirty and go to check our horses before riding out and there would be two or three reporters at the end of the lane waiting to talk with me about some aspect or other of the National and that went on for weeks. My mother, bless her, ended up censoring the papers that came in the house as the controversy mounted over whether or not a girl should ride in the National. I never actually knew about that until a couple of weeks before my second ride in the race on Martinstown in 1982 (she fell at the third) when I was clearing out some things in my mother's bedroom and came across a pile of papers she had hidden there; it was quite funny really, I had no idea about some of the things that had been written.

'There was the other side of the coin, of course, and I received between four and five hundred letters wishing me luck from people all over the country; and only two, both anonymous, really nasty letters but, typical of the way my mind works, I can remember word for word what those two letters said!

'I have to admit that Barony Fort loved and adored all the attention. He'd had a very bad stable habit, a stable vice called weaving which afflicts many nervous horses; they stand in a corner of the stable or lean over their door and shift from front foot to front foot and from side to side. It's not considered at all good for horses and Baron used to be a dreadful weaver. As time went on and I got increasingly uptight about the publicity, Baron became more blasé about the whole thing, gave up weaving and would walk out of his stable looking for the cameras, expecting to have his picture taken!

'My parents bought him for me from Richard Redgrave in Norfolk who said he was a perfect ride for a lady! In fact, he was anything but that, was 17.1 and inclined to jump to the right all the time as well as being rather headstrong. The crucial, deciding factor, however, was that he was a really superb jumper. I bashed round point-to-points on him week after week and he'd regularly finish second; he was extremely one-paced and not fast enough to win even a Lady's Open. We'd run every Saturday and I remember a friend saying one day, "There's more to training horses than you realise. You should build him up for a race, not run him one week and then bring him out fresh the following week." What happened? He had a week off and blew up the following week! That was Baron. But I only ever had one fall on him and after lady riders were granted licences, I was determined to have a bash round Aintree. He sailed round in the Foxhunters and I had no doubt in my heart that he could get round in the National.'

Ladbrokes, who were managing the National in 1977 for the second time,

Charlotte Brew leads Barony Fort
out of his stable at her parents' home
in Coggeshall, Essex, to meet the
demanding pressmen

promised Charlotte odds of 500–1 to a free £20 wager if she could complete the course – 'a) because they thought I'd never do it, and b) as an added incentive. And they were dead right; it was very much an added incentive!' Those odds tumbled to 8–1 on the day as Charlotte's friends piled cash on her and Barony Fort to survive the world's greatest steeplechase. 'I had a boy friend at the time who was a stockbroker in the City and he reckoned that a horse who had been round once was bound to complete the course. He persuaded his pals to heap on quite a lot of money and Ladbrokes said at the time that they stood to lose more if I got round than if Red Rum won!

'Red Rum's trainer Ginger McCain was, in fact, one of the loudest voices in the "a girl shouldn't ride in the National" lobby and by the time the meeting arrived, things had really got out of hand.

'It was then that I was most grateful to Ossie Dale, the man in charge of the stables at Aintree. He'd looked after my mother and me splendidly the previous year, in fact, I think he was quite taken with our completely dotty set up. He had selected ESB's box for Baron. The evening before the Foxhunters, I was mildly complaining about having to do my own horse when you always read about the National jockeys sitting in the sauna drinking champagne, so my mother went into Liverpool and returned with a bottle of champagne which we shared with Ossie, sitting on Baron's rug in his box. When we arrived the following year for the National, there was Ossie waiting to welcome us – with a bottle of champagne! It really made me feel at home after all the hassle.

'Baron was a bad traveller and we put him in our little horse-trailer and set off for Liverpool on the Wednesday so we were under Ossie's wing for three days. I was fascinated, sitting and listening to his tales of Aintree and greatly honoured when he asked me to sign his copy of the Grand National book written by Bill Curling and the late Clive Graham. Ossie gets all the jockeys who have won the race to sign – and then there's me. I was greatly honoured.

'Mother and I stayed at the Park Hotel right by the course which was ideal because none of the other trainers or jockeys were there and we were able to have some peace and quiet; I spent most of the Thursday and Friday in the stable block talking to Baron and listening to Ossie.

'*The News of the World*, who were sponsoring the National, had sent up two bodyguards to keep other pressmen away because they wanted my story for themselves and didn't want me to speak to anyone else. That was hilarious because I had a rather pretty young girl, Fiona Taylor, working for me at the time and she was with me at Aintree. The bodyguards stuck religiously to my side the first day and then they were hardly ever seen; they were too busy coping with Fiona!

'I rode Baron out for an hour on Thursday, Friday and Saturday mornings and took him right down to the bottom of the course where I could escape everyone,

A smile for the cameras from Barony
Fort in the parade before the
National

trying to run over a couple of press photographers on the way! By Friday night my
temper and nerves were indeed very frayed. That was when Ian Watkinson, who
was my big buddy at the time, really looked after me; he was fantastic. He
insisted that we went out the night before the race. We had a few dances and then
went on to a casino before I collapsed, exhausted, into bed around 2 a.m. I'm sure
it was the right thing to do; far better than going to bed early and tossing and
turning, trying to keep the National out of my mind.

'Next morning, after riding out and returning to the hotel for breakfast which,
in my case, was a cup of black coffee while the rest of the family tucked into bacon
and eggs, Ian walked the course with me and the reality of the whole thing really
began to sink in.

'There was no going back – and those fences, well, they're really something
else. Even though I'd ridden in the Foxhunters the previous year, I admit I began
to feel frightened as we walked round. I was struck not only by the size of the
fences, but by the angles. On television, they look as though they're all in a
straight line. They're not! They're all set at different angles and you notice that
walking the course.

'Ian could sense my tense mood and tried a little light relief as we approached

The Chair. God, that's fearsome. I'd never walked up so close to it before, I'd always maintained it was quite big enough to view from afar. We got within thirty feet and Ian said, "Come on, you are incredibly wet!" And with that he climbed in the ditch and pretended to be a mountaineer hauling himself out, much to the amusement of the crowd who had gathered around us. I told Ian he was tempting fate. What happened in the race? Ian had been prominent throughout the first circuit on Sage Merlin when he fell – at The Chair!

'The morning, thankfully, whizzed by and then it was time to change into my racing silks of light blue, cerise yoke and cap with white sleeves – and collect two smashing telegrams. One was from Captain Ryan Price, whom I had never met and who I consider very much to be the king pin; he's rather like the Clint Eastwood of racing, he doesn't give anything away and you never know what he's thinking. His message said: "Admire your pluck in running, best of luck, Ryan Price."

'The other telegram was from Bruce Hobbs who, in 1938 had, at seventeen, been the youngest rider ever to win the National; it was a tremendous honour to receive one from him, too. His message was: "I admire your pluck and determination and wish you all luck in running, Bruce Hobbs."

'Once the parade was over and we made our way down to the start, I was certainly aware of the noise; noise like I'd never heard before. I'd made up my mind exactly what I was going to do and how I was going to do it – whatever, I would get round safely. There was no way I was going down the inner. I knew my horse was too slow to win so the object was to go round quietly on the outside. I don't see any point in subjecting your horse to the extra drops which every fence has on the inner.

'At last we were off and I quickly settled at the back of the field. And Baron? He was loving all the excitement. He just cocked a hoof in the direction of the crowd and set off for the first fence. Marvellous! We made it . . . and on we went, up to Becher's, my, that was like jumping off the end of the world . . . then up came the Canal Turn, a fence that really worried me. Baron always jumped right and the Canal Turn is left but Richard Pitman had told me to "jump it at an angle and as you go past, take a bite out of the flag in the corner." I'm proud to say that's exactly what we did.

'On we went, over the fearsome Chair leaving poor old Ian running for cover, over the water and out into the country for the second time. By then, we were so far behind, people were cheering as we conquered each fence; I was loving every minute of it and determined to make it round. Baron, bless him, began to tire and as we approached the big, open ditch four from home I knew this was it – if we could make this we'd do it, but there was no way Baron could get over. We had four goes at it. If it had been one of the last three fences, we'd have done it for there were great big holes in them and we'd have scrambled through but there

Charlotte Brew and Barony Fort
clear Becher's – 'it was like jumping
off the end of the world'

was not a mark in that fence. It was sickening. If there'd been someone with a
chain-saw handy, I'd have cut a hole in the fence.

'I felt a terrible sense of anti-climax as we made our way back towards the
stables; I'd set my heart on getting round and we very nearly got there. Ossie and
my mother came rushing up as we approached the stables and they were over the
moon that we'd got so far, but I was disappointed.

'Ian, my parents, my brother Timothy, sister Sophie and everyone back at the
hotel, soon had me smiling again and we had a great party in the evening. Ian was
asked to account for his failure to hold on to his horse at The Chair. "I was
going to hold on," he said, "then I suddenly remembered the great big hooves of
Barony Fort were thundering along behind so I thought I'd better run for safety!"

'Well, we kept thundering along and to this day I defend my right to ride in the
race in the first place. Sure, it's a race and the object is to come first, but it's a race
in which anything can happen; that's why I was in the Grand National and not
the Gold Cup. My horse didn't stand a chance of winning but then neither did
Foinavon in 1967 and, looking at it in retrospect, Barony Fort had been round
Aintree and jumped the fences and I really felt he could get round. As it was, I was
the last person to go out, albeit almost a lap behind! But we almost made it . . .'

Whatever else, Charlotte Brew was the first woman to ride in the greatest
steeplechase in the world. No one can take that away from her.

John Buckingham

Never a week goes by without someone, somewhere, going up to John Buckingham and mentioning Foinavon and Buckingham, a warm, engaging man, would not want it any other way. When he is introduced to someone for the first time, it is always the same: 'This is John Buckingham, he won the Grand National on Foinavon.' And the reply inevitably goes like this: 'Oh, I remember: you were the lucky so-and-so who won when everything fell.' But Buckingham just smiles.

'People in racing, people who understand racing, they remember it rather differently. They realise you need a bit of luck to win the National. They understand.'

Not that Buckingham would dispute he had an extraordinary bit of luck that faraway Saturday, 8 April 1967, when, even by Grand National standards, the great race produced something quite incredible. The field approached the fence after Becher's second time round – the 23rd and one of the smallest on the circuit – with no hint of the drama to come when suddenly two loose horses started to run up and down the fence. There was instant pandemonium: there were horses and riders everywhere except going over the fence; there was nowhere for anyone to go even if they wanted to . . .

And suddenly there was Buckingham, having his first-ever National ride, and Foinavon, a 100–1 outsider, whose trainer had gone off to ride at Worcester and whose owner had stayed at home to watch the race on television, so remote his chance had seemed . . .

Ah yes, Buckingham remembers it well. 'I was about twentieth, jumping nicely but about 100 yards behind the leaders. I saw them all bunch up ahead of me and the nearer I got, the more I realised I would be among them if I didn't pull Foinavon to the right. Two loose horses were coming towards me as I lolloped towards the fence. I jerked him to the right and we were over.

'Up to that point, I'd been trying to stick somewhere near Josh Gifford on the favourite, Honey End. Indeed, he was only three lengths in front of me at the mêlé but, as it happened, he went straight for the middle of the fence. If I'd followed

Josh, there's no way I would have got through either.

'I couldn't believe that we had got over safely. Horses and jockeys were on the floor to the left of me and Stan Mellor, who had come off The Fossa, actually ran alongside me shouting, "Go on, Brod, you'll win!" I think he thought I was Paddy Broderick, who had been disputing the lead on Kirtle Lad before coming a cropper at the fence.

'You must admire Foinavon for getting over. He jumped that fence more or less in a canter yet I don't know what he must have thought of it all. There were horses galloping towards him, others whipping round, others rolling over, it was terrible, chaotic. Yet over he went and on we galloped . . .

'At that stage, I didn't know if anything else had jumped the fence before us and gone on. It wasn't until we'd cleared the Canal Turn and gone on towards Valentine's that I realised I was on my own. Out in front with every chance of winning the race of my dreams. I knew then that if I could keep the old fella on his feet, we'd win. My big worry was to keep him going. Any horse is tired after jumping four miles round Aintree and it's not made any easier when you're out on your own for as long as we were.

'But the old horse was marvellous and I only had to give him one clip with my stick. That was after jumping the last and I thought that Josh Gifford on Honey End and Terry Biddlecombe on Greek Scholar were getting a bit close.'

Buckingham and Foinavon galloped past the winning post at their own pace with many racegoers still frantically searching through the names of the forty-four runners to check that this most unlikely twosome had actually gone to post!

Gifford and Honey End, who had retreated fifty yards and started all over

The incredible chaos at the twenty-third in 1967: John Buckingham and Foinavon, top right, have somehow dodged it all and set off for one of the great surprises in the history of the National

John Buckingham and Foinavon pass the winning post at their own pace, with many racegoers still frantically searching through the names of the forty-four runners to check that this unlikely twosome had actually gone to post!

again before negotiating the 23rd, were second, beaten fifteen lengths with Red Alligator and Greek Scholar, both trained by Denys Smith, third and fourth. Amazingly no rider or horse was seriously hurt in the chaos and eighteen horses eventually completed the course.

It was a stunning, staggering, unbelievable National and the Stewards took the unprecedented step of making an announcement over the public address system to explain what had happened at the 23rd. The statement was: 'The Stewards want the racing public to know that in the Grand National two loose horses in the lead at the fence after Becher's refused. They baulked or brought down the majority of the field.'

Buckingham and Foinavon were the stuff from which Grand National fairy tales are made. Buckingham did not know what a horse looked like until he was fifteen when he went to work on the late Edward Courage's Oxfordshire estate. 'My mother had worked there as a dairy-maid and Mr Courage gave me the option of three jobs. I could have gone with the shepherd on the farm, with the gamekeeper, or in the stables. I chose the stables, though I'd never sat on a horse in my life.'

He was twenty-six when he rode Foinavon to victory, only his forty-fifth winner ever and eleventh of that season. He had ridden Foinavon just once before – in the Sunday Express Handicap Steeplechase at Cheltenham in the spring of 1966 – and was the sixth jockey to ride the horse in the 1966–67 season. The Grand National was Foinavon's sixteenth outing of the season and he had not won one.

Foinavon was, frankly, moderate to say the least. He was cast aside by Anne, Duchess of Westminster, in 1965 after Tom Dreaper had trained him to win three small chases in Ireland. Foinavon, then a seven-year-old, was sold for 2,000 guineas at Doncaster Sales to Cyril Watkins and his friend, Mac Bennellick. Bennellick gave Watkins his half of Foinavon in the September before the National, later saying ruefully: 'I was tightening up my finances and wanted to sell my half of Foinavon but no one wanted it so I gave it to Cyril. I was flabbergasted when the horse won the National.'

No more flabbergasted than Watkins who settled down in front of the television with his wife, Iris, at home in Finchampstead, Berkshire, to watch the race and could hardly believe his eyes. With a couple of jumps to go, he was too excited to sit still any longer and went for a walk in the garden to calm down. 'When I went back into the house, my wife was crying. We had won!'

Watkins, his wife, and three friends were just about the only people in the country to support Foinavon and won over £10,000 in bets. A spokesman for William Hill said at the time: 'It has been an absolute skinner for us. We could not have picked a better winner.' Ladbrokes reported: 'As a result of the National, we shall not have to pay out a single Spring double – not even a shilling

The most unlikely National heroes of all time – left to right: trainer John Kempton, his father who saddled Foinavon at Aintree, owner Cyril Watkins who stayed at home to watch the race on television, and Susie, the goat, Foinavon's constant companion

one.' The Tote returned Foinavon at an amazing 444–1.

Trainer John Kempton chose to ride at Worcester – he won on Three Dons – and watched the race on television there, and could not believe his eyes either. His father saddled Foinavon at Aintree. 'I thought he'd get round all right but I never thought he could win.'

Three jockeys turned down the ride on Foinavon before Kempton, who trained at Compton in Berkshire, telephoned Buckingham on the Wednesday before the race. 'I accepted the ride like a shot,' recalled Buckingham. 'Like every National Hunt jockey, I'd always wanted to ride in the National and I'd have ridden the horse for nothing. I went to Taunton on the Thursday to ride one for Mr Kempton and we had a chat about Foinavon then. There were no specific orders, just to do my best.'

The nearest Buckingham had been to the National at the time was as a stable lad for Edward Courage when he went to Liverpool with that grand old mare Tiberetta, who was third in 1957, second the following year and fourth in 1959. 'I've never seen a horse handle Liverpool as she did,' said Buckingham. 'There was no one to touch her for jumping Aintree. Even horses like Red Rum and Grittar, who were brilliant round there, could not, in my opinion, match Tiberetta for jumping ability.'

The late booking for Foinavon meant Buckingham had not arranged any digs but he and his brother Tom were squeezed into a boarding-house opposite Aintree where John had stayed as a stable lad. 'Tom slept on the sofa and I pulled together a couple of armchairs and slept on them. Not exactly the ideal preparation for the National!'

Foinavon's sleeping arrangements the night before were hardly conventional, either. He was a rather gregarious animal and arrived at Aintree accompanied by a goat named Susie. Unless Susie bedded down in Foinavon's box at night, the horse was liable to become rather disgruntled.

Buckingham was grateful for the early start on the morning of the race and strolled across to the racecourse 'to ride the old horse round a bit and renew acquaintance. Little did we know then what was in store for us. For one thing, I'd have made sure I was a bit fitter if I'd known earlier that I would have been riding in the National. I wasn't getting many rides at the time and to be racing fit, you need to be riding in a lot of races. I was riding work in the mornings for Mr Courage, of course, but that's not the same and I was mentally and physically shattered by the end of the National.

'It was several minutes before it sunk in that we'd won but by Saturday night I had no doubt whatsoever! I arrived at our house in Chipping Warden in Oxfordshire to find it all decked out with flags and bunting and the celebrations went on way into the early hours of Sunday morning down at the local. My wife, Ann, had watched the race on television with her grandparents in Leamington

John Buckingham going about his work as a jockeys' valet – never a week goes by without someone mentioning the 1967 National to him

and she was still in a state of shock when Tom and I arrived home. After all, we'd never considered I might win; I was just excited at riding in the National.'

Among those joining in the celebrations was former northern jump jockey Mick Bachelor, whose advice to Buckingham forty-eight hours earlier had been quite simply: 'Keep one leg each side and hope!'

Buckingham certainly kept one leg each side and hoped when all around him was chaos, but he has just one regret as he looks back on the greatest day of his life. 'Four years later, I was sure I was going to win again on Limeburner when I fell two out while in third place. I actually managed to remount and cross the line in twelfth place but there would have been no fluke about Limeburner winning. The horse had jumped magnificently and would have been a worthy winner. The ride was much less hard than I'd had on Foinavon and that's what makes me think I'd have won. You can tell how your horse is going by the way you feel yourself and I felt great!'

Buckingham, who had his best-ever season with twenty-one winners following Foinavon's triumph, rode four times in the National – he was twelfth on Limeburner in 1969 and sixth on Pride of Kentucky in 1970 – before retiring in the summer of 1971 to become a jockeys' valet.

Since then, he's twice 'done' the winning National jockey – Graham Thorner (Well To Do in 1972) and Charlie Fenwick (Ben Nevis in 1980). 'I thrill still to the electric atmosphere of the weighing-room on Grand National Day. You need to have experienced it to appreciate it. There are jockeys running round getting their racecards signed by all the other jockeys, everyone wishing each other good luck and, afterwards, the first thing every jockey says is the same, "Is everyone back safely?" Marvellous. I love it. I cannot imagine racing without the National.

'Mind you, Foinavon's National was, like so many, the "last" National and I don't mind admitting I was caught by a couple of crooks, whose type inevitably invade Aintree. These fellows were going round Liverpool selling a pamphlet for ten shillings which afterwards entitled you to a record of "the last Grand National"! I bought a couple and wrote away for them afterwards. I'm still waiting for my records. They must have made a fortune.'

But those two ten shilling notes were about all Buckingham lost that extraordinary day in 1967. Even now, he wonders just why fate singled him out. And like so many superstitious sportsmen – 'yes, I often wave at magpies' – one story nags away at the back of his mind.

'I'd been told that the first time Reynoldstown won the National in 1935, his owner and trainer, Major Noel Furlong, passed a funeral on the way to Aintree and the following year, he went round and round Liverpool until they saw a funeral. Now that is taking superstition a bit far. I don't say I'd do that, but when John Kempton rang me on the Wednesday to ask me to ride Foinavon, I was standing in the hall putting on a black tie as I was going to an uncle's funeral.'

Tommy Carberry

The other side of the National for Tommy Carberry as he parts company with Kilburn at the twenty-second in 1969. Steel Bridge and Richard Pitman are leading from the eventual winners, Highland Wedding and Eddie Harty, with The Fossa and Rondetto behind

Tommy Carberry reckoned he would need all the luck of the Irish if he was ever to get the dual Cheltenham Gold Cup winner L'Escargot safely around Aintree, never mind win the National.

With a grin, he recalled L'Escargot's first tilt at the race in 1972. 'The bookies made him 17–2 favourite but he took an instant dislike to the place. He was very slow over the first two fences and was almost stopping as we came to the third. There was a fallen horse just getting up as we went over. L'Escargot made no attempt to avoid it and just went straight for it. He ducked underneath the other horse's neck and I was knocked off. I thought then that if we were ever able to get

this fella round Liverpool, we'd be very lucky.'

But L'Escargot's trainer Dan Moore was a determined man and the horse's owner, American Raymond Guest, a former U.S. Ambassador in Dublin, was one of the legions who over the years dedicated themselves – many without success – to owning a National winner.

Guest had bought a number of horses to try to win the world's greatest steeplechase and failed every time. Then one day, Moore turned to him and said, 'Instead of trying to buy a horse to win the race, I think you have one in the yard to do it for you. I think L'Escargot can win a National.'

Carberry was not amused. L'Escargot's Gold Cup triumphs in 1970 and 1971 should have been followed, he felt, by a third Cheltenham victory – 'But he gave the race away going to the second last and we thought he'd begun to dislike racing a bit.' Hardly the right attitude for the hurly-burly of National Day and sure enough, as Carberry feared, L'Escargot did not want to know in 1972. 'I felt he was thinking, "I don't want any part of this racket!" He disliked Aintree straight away.'

Moore told Carberry, however, 'We'll try again next year but we'll need to get him to see things differently.' Moore decided to return to Aintree on 28 October for the William Hill Grand National Trial Handicap Chase and Carberry takes up the story once more.

'He was set to carry 12st 3lb and I reckoned we had no chance of getting round. It wasn't a question of his falling for he was a safe jumper, but I felt he'd be reluctant to go to Aintree. I was afraid he would remember his first visit and chuck it in again. The instructions were to school him round the place. Surprisingly to me, but not to Mr Moore, he jumped round splendidly and was only beaten into second place by Glenkiln, who was receiving 31lb.

'After that, there was nothing else but to try again in the 1973 National where he was once more set to carry 12st along with Fred Winter's great Australian horse, Crisp. L'Escargot jumped his way round adequately enough but I looked up on the second circuit and could see Crisp two fences in front; we had no chance of winning. Red Rum was about ten lengths in front of me and went after Crisp but L'Escargot was only just beginning to feel his way and although I made up a lot of ground after Becher's second time, we were never going to catch the other two and finished $25\frac{3}{4}$ lengths behind them. But at least we'd got round and it was a good introduction for the horse.

'I was more or less convinced then that he'd win a National and Mr Moore decided to train him specifically for the 1974 race and forget the Gold Cup in which L'Escargot had been fourth two weeks earlier.

'For my part, I was much happier and more relaxed about the horse. He had always been a careful jumper and that's essential at Aintree, and now we'd got him round and over those thirty fences, I was convinced we'd conquered any mental reluctance on his part. He had the class and speed to go wherever I put him in a race. I just had to pick him up, give him a kick and he was there. If there was a crowd in front of him, he'd watch out, take his time and pop the fence; he wouldn't throw a wild jump at it.

'I always felt that was the secret behind Red Rum. He went round Aintree like a rabbit. You couldn't knock him down even if you'd tied his legs together. He was ready for anything. They say an Aintree horse needs five legs – I'd say Red Rum had nine! No matter what he was doing, how he met those fences, it was all so easy to him, he danced his way round Aintree.

'Unfortunately for me, Red Rum danced his way round in 1974 even though he carried 23lb more than the previous year and L'Escargot had 1lb less at 11st 13lb. Red Rum hit the 26th and should have gone, but he didn't and ran on too strongly for us. We were second and I left the track that night convinced I'd never win the blasted race after all.

'But back we went in 1975, this time with only 11st 3lb to carry while Red Rum once again had 12st. It's amazing how time heals; by the day of the National, 5 April, I was confident that this time, we'd win it. I think it's a big advantage to be on a horse in the National that has been round before and history proves that time and again; horses go back to Aintree and run well. L'Escargot had even begun to enjoy the place and was looking for a battle again.

'There was a delay at the start in '75 because one horse had spread a plate. I dismounted and I remember leaning over the rail chatting with Jeff King, who was on Money Market, and saying to him, "With a bit of luck, I'll win!" Luckily Mick Ennis, who looked after the horse, was down at the start and led L'Escargot round as the minutes ticked away. That's a tense moment in any National and a delay adds to the pressure; I'm always uptight before a race like that and was pleased Mick was there to look after the horse.

'Eventually, we were off and all was well until L'Escargot, amazingly, made a mess of the 7th second time round, one of the smallest fences on the course. He hit it a right thump and almost dislodged me; I lost my irons and landed with my arms around his neck. I was lucky to get back in the plate. My heart sank and I thought that there must be something wrong with him because he just couldn't be right to do that. He'd never hit a fence like that before. I decided to give him the next two fences and see how he went. I was afraid I might have to pull him up. He came up with the right answer, however, flying them both. We were on our way again and this time we would not be caught.

'As we jumped the fourth last with Red Rum, Brian Fletcher turned to me and said, "Go on, Tommy, you've won a minute!" L'Escargot was going so easily, I, too, felt sure we'd make it this time. I wanted to keep with Red Rum as long as possible because L'Escargot was a horse that I dared not take to the front a mile from home in case somebody came to challenge us and put us under pressure;

L'Escargot makes an uncharacteristic mistake and almost unships Tommy Carberry at the seventh second time round in 1975, but Carberry kept the horse going to victory

there was always a nagging doubt that he might not run on again. But there were no worries that day and we sailed home by fifteen lengths, Grand National winners at last!'

Raymond Guest had announced in the parade ring before the race that he was giving L'Escargot to Dan Moore's wife, Joanie. After the race, he was obviously thrilled. 'I've been trying for twenty years to win this race,' he said, 'and I owe everything to Dan Moore and Tommy Carberry.'

L'Escargot had made Raymond Guest a very happy man and added one more triumph to the long line of successes Carberry has enjoyed ever since he burst on to the racing scene as Ireland's champion Flat apprentice in 1958. 'There are probably easier ways of earning a living,' said Carberry, 'but it's a great life.'

It is a life not without its downs though and he chuckled over two National memories with less happy endings. 'My first ride, on the thirteen-year-old Mr What in 1963, ended with me lying face down in the ditch at Valentine's first time round, with a couple of horses trotting up and down the ditch; it was a bit overawing at the time!'

Then, in 1977 on his first National ride since L'Escargot's triumph, Carberry only got as far as the first where he was brought down on War Bonnet. 'It was

Top: Tommy Carberry and L'Escargot take the final fence just ahead of Brian Fletcher and Red Rum before going on to win at the fourth time of trying in 1975

Below: An overjoyed Raymond Guest leads in L'Escargot

terribly disappointing after building myself up and getting the adrenalin going. I'd walked the complete track twice – all I really needed to have done was go as far as the first!'

The memory of L'Escargot succeeding at the fourth time of asking, however, outweighs all else for the carefree Carberry, without doubt one of the finest jockeys ever to enter the winner's enclosure at Aintree.

Dave Dick

In 1956, Dave Dick was invited to meet the Queen Mother minutes after riding ESB to victory in the most talked about, argued over National of all – minutes after the Queen Mother's Devon Loch had collapsed fifty yards from the winning post with the crowd already hailing a Royal victory . . .

'Well done, Dick,' said the Queen Mother. 'What did you think when you saw my horse had collapsed ahead of you?'

'I was delighted, Ma'am,' said Dick, who tells the story with that mischievous glint in his eye, and added, 'I'd really put my foot in it, of course. Poor old Lord Sefton shuddered and said, "Right oh, Dick, that will be all, thank you very much."'

Of course, Dick *was* delighted to have won the National at his sixth attempt though he readily admitted, 'I was just lucky, unbelievably lucky. When Devon Loch came alongside me at the second last, his tongue was hanging out and it was completely black; he looked to me as if he'd gone. I thought he was exhausted. Funny thing though, as he jumped the last, he flew away from me and I just dropped my hands; I had no chance of catching him. I couldn't believe it when he sank to the ground. I nearly rammed him in the backside. I felt desperately sorry for the Queen Mother, who has done so much for racing.'

Dick refuses to attempt to analyse what went wrong with Devon Loch in that unbelievable moment. 'My horse, ESB, never got the National trip. He was always gone between the second last and the last and I rode him twice more in the following two years and never felt we'd win again.'

That victory ensured Dick his own place in racing history as the only man to have ridden the winner of both the National and the Lincoln which he won in 1941 on Gloaming before weight problems to his six-foot frame forced him to quit riding on the Flat.

Dick, fun-lover extraordinaire, lit up the National thirteen times, finishing second on Mont Tremblant in 1953, third on Wot No Sun in 1952 and failing to complete only four times. He was a brilliant horseman and had few peers round Aintree – and few equals when it came to enjoying himself away from the track.

Dave Dick prepares for the world's greatest steeplechase – he rode thirteen times in the National and had few peers round Aintree

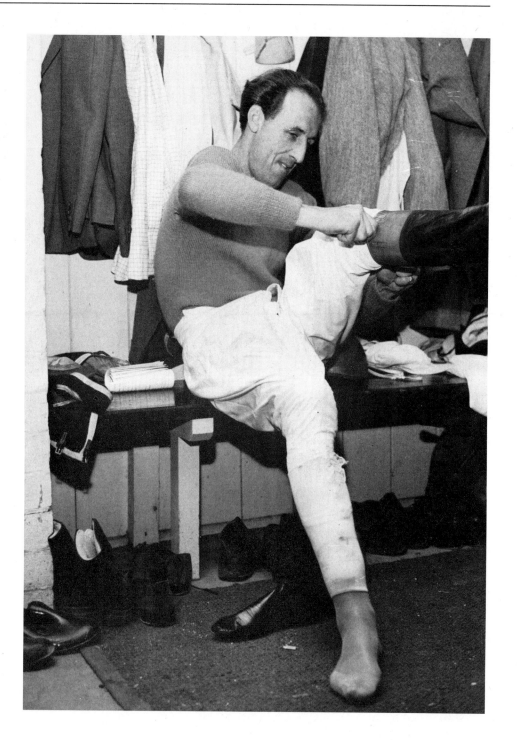

Dave Dick shows his delight as he passes the winning post on ESB, but the spectators are looking back to the stricken Devon Loch

At the start of one National, he eyed a banner inscribed: 'Your sins will find you out'. 'If that's the case,' said Dick, 'I shan't get as far as the first.' Dick always got as far as the first and beyond and feels he would have put the record straight in 1965 – his last National – and won on Kapeno but for listening to the advice of John Lawrence, now Lord Oaksey!

'I would have loved to have won another National on true merit,' recalled Dick, 'and Kapeno would have done it for me. I always blame John for that. He rode Kapeno in his three races before the National and told me, "Whatever you do, sit still on him. Don't ask him for a jump." Well, it's a helluva long way to go round Aintree without asking a horse for one. I mean, that's half the fun of it. Anyway, I never asked Kapeno the whole way round the first circuit; then we jumped the 17th and 18th and got to the big ditch. I remember thinking to myself, "I wonder if you can stand off?" and I gave him the office. He was absolutely brilliant. I thought we would win 100 yards.

'We jumped the next two and came to Becher's. Then I thought to myself,

Michael Scudamore and Oxo clear the last before going on to victory in 1959. The celebrations after his win were quite something

"Shall I take any notice of that Lawrence or shan't I?" But I was obviously too busy thinking and the horse was too busy thinking, and we both did nothing; we just galloped straight on, we never left the ground. He was obviously waiting for me to give him a kick, and I was waiting for him to jump! If I'd ridden him just like any other horse and given him a kick, I feel sure we'd have gone on and won.

'Mind you, if I hadn't done what John had told me, I'd probably have ended up on the floor early on!'

Pas Seul, Dick's ride in the previous year's National – 'one horse who would have beaten Arkle,' Dick claimed – also 'went straight on' and discovered that is one thing you cannot get away with at Aintree. 'He was a great horse, but he used to do that on park courses; he just went straight on. He moved the whole fence; it takes a bit of moving, but that's what he did to the 12th at Aintree. He moved the frame of the fence, and pushed the bottom of the fence out – but still he never fell. He was on the floor the other side, with me still sitting on him but he never turned over. When I stepped off him, he was sitting there like a dog on the floor – he'd knocked himself out!'

Dick and his pals, men like Fulke Walwyn, Tim Molony, Tim Brookshaw and Michael Scudamore, were a knock-out wherever they went and the Adelphi

Hotel in Liverpool annually rocked to their merry making. 'It was all good fun, a gas in those days and we were like a lot of kids.'

But the celebrations after Scudamore won on Oxo in 1959 were quite something even by their standards. Dick laughed at the memory.

'We were going well and Scu was sipping his gins and tonics and dropping the empty glasses out of the window off the top floor of the Adelphi; then another one and another. The next thing we knew was when the door flew open and about eight policemen came rushing in. "Who's throwing glasses out of the window?" they demanded to know. Scu said, "I am – watch!" and dropped another one. The coppers just stood there, they couldn't believe it. A syphon followed the glass down – I think that went through a taxi! Anyway, the police gave him a bollocking and had a drink with us! They were great up at Liverpool.'

Those were the days. 'Days when the fences really were tough,' insisted Dick. 'They've spoilt it all now and softened it as a start. You get a lot of horses going round Liverpool who wouldn't have got round fifteen or twenty years ago; if you hit the fences in those days, you went back the same way you came!'

For all his pride in years gone by, his admiration for riders of his generation, men like his life-long friend Fred Winter – they were at school together in Ewell, Surrey – Dick has no hesitation in naming a modern-day jockey as the best he has seen round Liverpool. 'I've never seen anyone ride Aintree better than John Francome, he's brilliant.' Praise indeed from one of the finest National riders of all time.

Dick Francis

'You start the season on 1 August and everything you think about is the Grand National the following spring. What am I going to ride in the National, has it a chance? The number of times you say to a trainer, "This is a great Liverpool horse, I'd love to ride him in the National." Looking forward to a great ride in the National, dreaming of winning, I think that's all the better jockeys think about . . . the National is the pinnacle of the whole season.'

Those are the words of Dick Francis, former champion National Hunt jockey, ex-Royal jockey and now thriller writer extraordinaire. A man on whom the Grand National played its cruellest trick.

Eight times Francis went to the starting gate but he never once came back a winner though his eighth and final attempt in 1956 remains one of sport's heartbreak stories. Fifty yards from the winning post, Francis and the Queen Mother's Devon Loch were out in front, sure to win, when the ten-year-old completely collapsed. ESB and Dave Dick went past to claim the victory Dick Francis wanted so badly.

The scene has been relayed around the world countless times; more words have been written about it than Dick Francis has poured into his best-sellers. 'What a burden to carry to my grave,' smiled this genial man ruefully as he settled down to recall his National memories once more.

You may feel they are filled with heartache and ill luck but Dick bears no malice. 'Aintree was, and is still, my favourite racecourse. I loved riding there.'

Dick's first ride in the National was on 26 March 1949. 'I finished second on Roimond behind George Owen's Russian Hero which was particularly sad for me because Russian Hero was the first horse I ever rode when I went into racing in October 1946. That was the Woore Hunt meeting and I'd only been with George about a week when he said I could ride Russian Hero in the Knighton Novices Chase. We finished fourth and I subsequently rode Russian Hero several more times.

'I intended to remain an amateur until the end of the 1949 season and was

The slow-motion agony of Dick Francis and Devon Loch as the Queen Mother's horse collapses fifty yards from the winning post

Roimond leads the parade in front of the packed stands in 1949, the first National for Dick Francis

delighted to be asked to ride in most of the important amateur chases which come at that time of the year. But the Stewards of the National Hunt Committee had other ideas. When I arrived at Cheltenham, they asked to see me and, in a friendly way, pointed out that I was riding so much for no fee that I was possibly taking rides away from professional jockeys who depended on them for their livelihood. Would I either, they said, ride only in amateur races in future, or become a professional and compete fairly for my rides.

'I asked to be allowed to go on as before until the end of the season and, at first, I thought they would agree but they changed their minds and decided that I must become a professional at the end of that week.

'So that was that. But I never regretted the decision for one moment because from then on I was getting paid for doing something I loved. I was immediately offered a job for the following season with Lord Bicester – a fantastic opportunity because he had the most powerful string of horses in the country at the time. And he offered me the 1949 National ride on the top weight, Roimond, who was to carry 11st 12lb.

'My first National! It was quite a moving experience. I thought that the nervous excitement I felt before I went out to ride Roimond was because it was my first National, but I felt it every year afterwards. It was a fantastic sight. In those days, about 250,000 people came to Aintree and I remember looking up as I led the parade down and seeing those masses of people in the stands, all with their eyes on us.

'Roimond gave me a wonderful ride. I even dreamed at one stage that I might win but it was an impossible task trying to give 18lb to Russian Hero. I knew we were done for at Becher's second time round when Larry McMorrow and Russian Hero loomed up alongside me; they were going like a bomb. I thought, "He's got his second wind, we'll never catch him." And I didn't. I plugged on just hoping that Russian Hero would make a mistake but, knowing the horse so well, I feared the worst. Even so, second in my first National, I was happy enough but exhausted. So exhausted in fact that I could hardly walk when I got off Roimond; he was such a big horse, incredibly wide, my legs were so stiff that I had great difficulty walking with my saddle into the weighing-room.

'Russian Hero's victory was a great triumph for Cheshire and I was still living there at the time. The winner was owned and bred by Fernie Williamson, who was reputed to have had £10 on the horse at 300–1. And, of course, the horse was trained at Malpas by my mentor George Owen, whose advice about Aintree I never forgot.

'Before my first ride at Aintree, he told me to go and walk round the course – in the opposite direction. Those fences looked really big, far worse on your feet . . . and so different when you come back the right way on a horse! You even start thinking that they are almost easy!

'If I'd stayed with George instead of taking Lord Bicester's retainer, I'd have ridden Russian Hero in the 1949 National, but I was delighted to be invited to join in the celebrations that evening. Fernie Williamson invited all his friends to an hotel in Chester and asked if I would propose the health of Larry McMorrow. I hate having to speak in public but agreed nonetheless. And when I got on my feet, I took the gathering back to one night the previous December . . .

'At that time, I was still assistant trainer to George Owen. He ws away at the Newmarket Sales. I went round with the feed wagon that night – George always fed his horses late, at about ten o'clock – and when I reached Russian Hero's box, he was down with colic. I got his lad up and Mrs Owen telephoned the vet to come out; he arrived and told us to keep walking the horse round. Well, the lad and I walked Russian Hero round and round until dawn by which time the colic had passed. He was right again in a few days, having just a short while off, and George had him 100 per cent for Aintree.

'But I told the party that night: "A few weeks ago, the lad and I were walking this horse round the stables all night; if I'd known what he was going to do today, I'd have let the bugger die!"'

Francis was back on Roimond for the 1950 National and they were made 10–1 joint favourites with Freebooter, the eventual winner. 'Roimond was a good horse but he had so many off days,' recalled Francis, 'and that was one of them. He'd jumped Aintree brilliantly in 1949, but he gave me a dreadful ride the following year. He wasn't going to have a go that day and we fell at the fence after Becher's on the first circuit. He was a bit of a mule, a pig of a horse really.'

The 1951 National saw Francis on Finnure. 'He was one of the best horses I ever rode, and certainly the best I ever rode in the National. I'd won the final running of the Champion Chase on him at Aintree in 1950 and after that I really thought we'd win the National for he had jumped brilliantly.

'But the 1951 National was the year the starter let us go before everyone was ready and there was chaos at the first fence where twelve of the thirty-six runners departed – including Finnure. It was a dreadful feeling. We were in mid-air and I could see several horses on the floor already and thought, "God, how am I going to miss them?" Finnure jumped the fence beautifully, side-stepped to miss one of the fallen horses as he landed but slipped up, twisting a hock. It was a great catastrophe.

'Worse still. I could have ridden the winner, Nickel Coin, if I'd been available. Both the owner and trainer asked me, but I was committed to Finnure.'

Francis survived only to the 7th on Skyreholme in Teal's 1952 National, and the following year rode Senlac Hill – 'the worst jumper I ever rode. He'd given me some terrible falls on ordinary racecourses, never mind Aintree, and put me in hospital at Cheltenham and Newbury. Lingfield was the only place I used to win on him. However, he was qualified for the National and Lord Bicester, naturally, wanted to have a go. The bookies even offered 50–1 against Senlac Hill just getting round because of his aversion to open ditches. I dreaded it and told Lord Bicester we'd never get past the third fence, the first open ditch. I always regarded that as a major obstacle; once you were over that, you could reckon on enjoying yourself.

'We got to the third and survived – he rattled it but got over. He kept rattling them and came round to The Chair where he made the most almightly noise as he rapped the wooden guard rail. I couldn't believe it when I found myself on the other side – and still on Senlac Hill! By then we were getting further and further behind the remaining runners but I knew I dare not pull up; Lord Bicester would not have been amused. So we kept going, somehow negotiating the fences until we came back on to the racecourse for the second time, the last of five survivors and about half a fence behind the other four.

'We finished all right, officially a bad fifth behind Early Mist, Mont Tremblant, Irish Lizard and Overshadow. Lord Bicester was delighted. I could hardly believe it and the radio commentator Raymond Glendenning certainly couldn't. He was naming the first, second, third and fourth for the listeners, adding, "That's all there are to finish – oh, no, there's another coming up now. Oh, it's Senlac Hill, he must have fallen and is just cantering in!" Ironically, Lord Bicester had been the

Twelve jockeys were unseated at the first in 1951. Left ro right: Paddy Fitzgerald (Texas Dan), Bryan Marshall (Land Fort), Dick Francis (Finnure), Mr Bob McCreery (Stalbridge Rock), Jack Dowdeswell (Cadamstown) and Mr Michael Scudamore (East A'Calling) watch the race from afar

under-bidder for Early Mist at the dispersal sale following the death of J. V. Rank.

Francis ended up on 40–1 outsider Icy Calm in 1954. 'I was going to ride one for Lord Bicester but at the last moment the horse didn't run and George Archibald rang and said he'd give me a nice present to ride Icy Calm, who was very small but had a reputation for being a good jumper in France.

'I was walking round at the start near Arthur Thompson who leaned over and said, "We've got no chance. We'll let them go and run round together at the back and enjoy ourselves." I readily agreed. We went round together all right, jumping the first three fences in front! I remember jumping that first open ditch and Arthur yelling, "What the hell are we doing here?" I carried on enjoying myself until I was forced to pull up at the 19th but Arthur and Southern Coup kept going and were eighth of the nine finishers.'

In 1955, Francis fell at the first for the second time – on Mariner's Log. And so to Saturday 24 March 1956 and Devon Loch . . .

'I've never wavered in my belief that the noise frightened Devon Loch and caused him to collapse. From the last fence onwards, the cheers which greeted us were tremendous and growing louder with every yard we went and although I

Seconds before the agony – hats are off ready to salute the Queen Mother's Devon Loch and Dick Francis. Front row, left to right: Princess Margaret, H.M. Queen Elizabeth, the Princess Royal, Mrs Cazalet, Peter Cazalet, H.M. Queen Elizabeth the Queen Mother

knew the reason for them, they may have been puzzling and confusing to Devon Loch, who could not know that his owner was a queen.

'In order to hear better what was going on, he would make a horse's instinctive movement to do so and into those newly pricked and sensitive ears fell a wave of shattering intensity. The noise that to me was uplifting and magnificent may have been exceedingly frightening to Devon Loch. He may have tried to throw himself backwards away from it; he may have reacted to it in the same convulsive way a human being jumps at a sudden loud noise, and a severe nervous jerk at such a stage in the race could certainly have been enough to smash the rhythm of his stride and bring him down.

'The weather records show that there was a light breeze blowing that day from behind the stands and this must have carried the huge sound with it. I remember how startled I was when I first heard the cheers for the Queen Mother's horse M'as-tu-vu at Lingfield and they were a whisper compared with the enveloping roar at Liverpool. So I think one must seriously consider whether Devon Loch may not have been struck down by the public joy.'

Francis was a forlorn figure that day as he walked away from disaster. No one

Seconds after the agony – Dick Francis stoops to pick up his whip, Devon Loch is back on his feet and the heartache has only just begun

in the history of the National has been so near and yet so far from victory.

He never rode in the race again. 'I was very hopeful at the time that I'd ride in the National again and hopeful, too, that it would be on Devon Loch. But he broke down before the 1957 race and Lord Abergavenny, the Queen Mother's National Hunt adviser, suggested then would be the time for me to hang up my boots. I'd never given the idea a moment's thought but I took his advice. Looking back, I might never have taken up writing but for the Devon Loch incident. My autobiography was a huge success and I've never looked back, my writing has taken me all over the world.'

Does Francis feel that the National was cruel to him? 'Certainly not. I don't think it was unkind to me at all. I was just unlucky. I have always thought it was the greatest race in the world and I still do.'

A six-inch piece of wood inscribed 'Dick Francis, Aintree 1956' is one of his most treasured possessions. Presented to him by the Stratford Racecourse Supporters' Club, it was shaved off the actual winning post at Aintree. 'That means a lot to me, it was a nice thing to receive.' A reminder of a race Dick Francis will never be allowed to forget . . . and nor would he wish to.

John Oaksey

There are few journalists who could even contemplate riding in the Grand National, and even fewer who could take part and then within minutes of weighing-in, climb the well-worn stairs to the Aintree Press room, pick up the telephone and dictate a thousand-word plus rider's eye-view account of it all.

But then Lord Oaksey is no ordinary hack but a racing correspondent whose feel and understanding for the sport comes over in every piece he writes.

That was surely never better illustrated than in his account of the National in the *Sunday Telegraph* on 31 March 1963, dictated, amazingly, within minutes of John Lawrence, as he was at the time, finishing second on Carrickbeg to Ayala, a heart-breaking second for he was passed just yards from the winning post he yearned for.

'That race remains my greatest National memory,' said John, 'for I always feel you remember better those things you have actually taken part in though I did also ride in the greatest National of all, when Red Rum defeated Crisp in 1973.' John was seventh that year on Proud Tarquin. Fate decreed that he was never to improve on Carrickbeg's second, though he fell only four times in eleven National rides and was ninth on both Crobeg in 1964 and Regimental seven years later.

This is how Ayala ended John's lifetime ambition – and this amazing account is exactly how it appeared on the Sunday morning breakfast table the following day:

Three-quarters of a mile from home today the dream of a lifetime seemed to be coming true before my eyes. 'Go on John, you'll win' – and the speaker, as I passed him before the second last was Pat Buckley on Ayala. He thought it was true, too. But half a minute later as Carrickbeg and I tired together in the final desperate fifty yards, it was he and Mr P. B. Raymond's [Teasy Weasy] gallant chestnut who dashed our hopes.

It was, I think, setting out on the second circuit that the thought of victory first entered my head. Carrickbeg had long since made the fences look and feel like hurdles and, after jumping the water well behind, he moved up

Standing room only for George Slack as he parts company with Kingstel at Becher's in 1961. John Lawrence and Taxidermist, centre, are also about to fall

outside his field turning away from the stands with a surge of power that warmed my heart.

At Becher's the second time, he made one of the few mistakes I remember and, for an awful moment, his big brave head seemed to rest on the quarters of another horse stumbling in front of us. But then, somehow, we were clear and at The Canal, as Ayala blundered badly, Carrickbeg nipped inside him, like a polo pony.

Now there were only a handful ahead and, as the fences flicked by, we pulled them back one by one, until four from home, when for the first and only time in this hectic, wonderful race, fate took a hand against us. Out and About had been in front from the start but now three lengths ahead of Carrickbeg he ploughed low through the fence and fell. Seeing him go my horse, for once, failed to pick up when I asked and, as he landed in a sprawling heap, had to swerve and struggle round his fallen rival. At the time it did not seem to matter for, coming on to the racecourse, I saw Gerry Scott pick up his whip on Springbok. The favourite could do no more and, before the second last, we were past both him and Ayala, upsides in front with Hawa's Song, and the stands looming ahead like the shores of a promised land.

It was a sight that has been with me day and night for months – and now, seen in reality, will never, never be forgotten. You can only just hear the

crowd, a murmur from afar, and the thing I remember best is a big chunk torn out of the last fence – and thinking whatever happens I must steer clear of that.

But Carrickbeg made no mistakes. I can't remember how he jumped it – but there we were, safe on the flat – and the winning-post still a hundred miles away. Until now I had not felt tired. The horse had done it all and still, halfway up the run-in, as we straightened round the final elbow, he was strong and galloping under me.

At this stage, Pat Buckley told me later, he never thought Ayala could get there. As for me, he might have been in another world – all that mattered was the post, nearer and nearer now he strived by agonising strides.

But then it happened – nothing much, invisible perhaps from the stands – but there, fifty yards from home, I felt Carrickbeg sprawl and change his legs. The rhythm was gone and hard as I strove to pull him together, the last dreg of his strength – and mine – had drained away.

It still seemed possible – but then, like Nemesis, the worst sight I ever expect to see on a racecourse. Ayala's head appeared at my knee. He and Pat Buckley had never given up and must have struggled like heroes to make up four lengths from the last.

Above: Lord Oaksey, whose love of National Hunt racing shines through all he writes

Opposite: John Lawrence and Carrickbeg take the final fence in front in 1963 (*top*) but they are caught and passed in the final yards by Pat Buckley and Ayala (*bottom*)

But they did – and poor Carrickbeg, with no more help available from me, staggered home gasping, his job gallantly done, the prize so very nearly his. Seven years old, a mere beginner by chasing standards, he had run the race of a lifetime – and there will perhaps, be other years. But whether there are or not, I will never, never forget the ride he gave me today, the instant ungrudging way he answered my call, his strength and courage when things went wrong, his featherlight agility when they didn't.

* * *

The hours and minutes before a National are always hell and today, when we left the warm dark haven of the weighing-room, a cruel wind bit through thin breeches to drive one's heart deeper still into one's boots. Threading through the crowd towards the ring, every word of encouragement is welcome. Today Bobby Petre was one of those to wish me luck – and since he was the last amateur to win (Lovely Cottage in 1946) – I took it gratefully as an omen of good fortune.

The huge field took even longer than usual to sort into line and all the time, striving to keep your fingers warm, cold, stiffness and fear made it hard indeed to smile. 'Hope you get something to write about,' someone said.

'Who's coming with me on the outside?' Dave Dick, as usual, sounded cheerful – and I followed him to the right of the field alongside Terry Biddlecombe on Wingless. Starter Alec Marsh, who knows how it feels, did not keep us waiting long and soon the Melling Gate flashed by with the first green and grim ahead.

I did not see Magic Tricks fall there and, tracking Mr Jones in the second group, Carrickbeg jumped it like a bird. He hit the third and that more than anything filled me with confidence for his head came up instead of down, like the safety net on an aircraft carrier.

Becher's was nothing – a soaring joy with scarcely even a pause on landing – but at the 10th a ghastly crash beside me spelt the end for Connie II, a harsh reminder that this was no happy-go-lucky picnic. Mostly they seemed to be jumping well (twenty-two finished, so they must have) but as Out and About led us past the stands, The Chair loomed up and Wingless, riderless in front of Carrickbeg, gave me a nasty moment.

But all was well and now, I thought, it's time to get a bit closer. Michael Scudamore told me he tried to follow on O'Malley Point as Carrickbeg made his ground but couldn't – and galloping up the middle to get the clearest possible view, we closed on the leaders stride by stride.

I think it was Loyal Tan on whose back we so nearly landed over Becher's. He had up till then given Terry Biddlecombe a wonderful ride – an example, like Carrickbeg himself, of how a horse who ran deplorably last time out can rise above himself on the day.

As if remembering The Canal from first time round, Carrickbeg swerved like a boomerang in mid-air and, without help from me, got a couple of priceless lengths. It was here that Pat Buckley must have sat tight as sticking plaster for Ayala carved a hole big enough for a London bus. Springbok, I think, was just behind me at this stage but I really cannot say for sure. From then on, you see, it was all a marvellous jumbled dream – a dream that only became a nightmare seconds before the dawn.

Of those I did see in the last mile, Hawa's Song must have run a wonderful race, brilliantly justifying Willie Stephenson's last-minute purchase. Springbok, surprisingly for so stout a stayer, did not quite see it through and little French Lawyer who had jumped like a stag actually got in front until his stamina gave out just before the racecourse.

Frenchman's Cove, too, had jumped well in his blinkers but from The Chair Dave Dick was never really hopeful. Pat Taaffe 'thought I might be placed' just after The Canal but Owen's Sedge was badly baulked there by loose horses and what chance he had was gone. For Team Spirit, the pace was always just too hot. He plugged on bravely to be fourth but Willie Robinson could never get him near enough to strike a real blow.

Ayala has not been easy to train and to get him ready on so light a preparation for such a gruelling marathon was a real triumph for Keith Piggott – Lester's father.

Richard Pitman

Richard Pitman's Grand National routine never varied during his riding days . . . a few jars at a Southport hotel on Friday night, up at the crack of dawn on Saturday morning to travel to Aintree and exercise his horse, back to the hotel for breakfast, a mid-morning sweat and glass of champagne in the sauna at Southport, then a few minutes in church on the way back to the racecourse.

Why call into church? 'It was insurance, I think. You are always covering eventualities – in case you lost your head and never came round again; it helps your peace of mind. I suppose it sounds a bit like a joke but I've heard jockeys pray during the National, especially when they've got a chance . . .

'They'll approach a fence and say, "God, let me get over this one." It's a sort of "let me get over this one and I'll do whatever you want in the future". I've heard that many times. A lot of very hard men have asked for a little bit of help from the Almighty.'

We could be forgiven for thinking that Pitman's prayers were not answered on 31 March 1973 when Pitman and his magnificent partner, Crisp, were caught and passed in the last few strides by Red Rum. They were denied victory after leading from Becher's first time round . . . after jumping so magnificently, so aggressively . . . after humping round 12st against Rummy's 10st 5lb.

Not a bit of it. 'They say it's no good being a loser. But in my guts, I've got things that will last me forever – how we went to Becher's for example, saw a long stride, stood off and got away with it, without hardly pecking. Marvellous! The memories come flooding back of those fantastic leaps; many rich men would pay a fortune to get a thrill like that . . .

'I was desperately sorry immediately afterwards for Crisp's owner, Sir Chester Manifold, a grand old man who should have had a National winner; for Fred Winter, what an ace trainer and a wonderful man; for Chippy Chape, the lad who did the horse – he loved that horse as if it was his wife, or child, part of the family; for the millions of punters who had made Crisp the joint 9–1 favourite with Red Rum. They were all losers, but I wasn't, I was the only winner . . . I had had an experience that will last me to my grave.'

It was an experience Pitman loves to re-live: 'I urged Crisp into immediate action tight to the inside rails where only the better jumpers dare to go. It is a fair run to the first fence with most riders trying to get a good look at it. Crisp saw the first fence, took a hold of his bit and accelerated towards it. If Fred Winter had waved a thousand pound note in front of me, there was no way I would have been able to stop for it. I checked Crisp's stride the moment he landed.

'To my surprise he responded for twenty yards or so before catching sight of the next fence, then going at it as if he wanted to eat it. I realised I would unbalance him if we fought too much so I just kept hold of his head until inside the massive wings of the fence where I gave him the office to jump. It was obvious that until the edge had gone off him, he would have the upper hand going into a fence, making it imperative that I had control on landing. Had he not responded, his headlong dash from fence to fence would have resulted in utter exhaustion after a mile and a half.

'The third fence at Aintree is greatly under-estimated. It is as big as The Chair and comes after two small fences, catching the cocky horse or rider by surprise. I felt wonderful as Crisp sailed over it with utter contempt. He had shown me his Aintree potential and instilled all the confidence I needed to be as brave as he. It is vital that both horse and rider be on a par with each other.

'Crisp accelerated towards Becher's, meeting it just right, powered into the air and soared over the top. His jump took me further away from the fence than I had ever been before which made the enormous drop on landing seem like eternity. It was like stepping into the unknown, expecting your legs to be snatched away at any second. He didn't peck on landing as most horses do in order to counterbalance their speed and surprise at finding no ground to land on at the normal height.

'I had by then gone several lengths clear without increasing my speed, my passage round the inner beginning to tell. The track at the Canal Turn runs away at right angles to the fence making it necessary to jump across it rather than straight. With no other horse around, Crisp was able to do my bidding and a superb cross jump, causing my foot to brush the wing, enabled us to increase our lead still further.

'On towards The Chair. It has a yawning ditch on the take-off side of a 5ft 6in thorn fence with the ground slightly raised on the landing side, ready to trip up any unbalanced horse. Crisp flicked the top of the fence as if to test its might and without further ado headed for the water.

'Grey Sombrero, the nearest rival, was already some fifteen lengths back, and fell at this point, leaving us fully twenty-five lengths clear of the pack. Could the two-miler Crisp keep up this gallop for another two and a quarter miles? Alternatively, were we too far clear to be caught? For the last ten fences, the noise of my pursuers had been diminishing until now I was alone. It was quite eerie.

Richard Pitman and Chippy Chape with Crisp. 'Chippy loved that horse as if it was his wife,' said Pitman

'As we jumped our way down to Becher's second time, the relics of the first circuit were to be seen everywhere. Great holes in some of the fences told tales of heavy falls and shattered dreams. A bridle that had been wrenched off a horse's head as he trod on the dangling reins when he tried to get up on his feet, lay broken on the grass. Horseless jockeys leaned on the rails, their chance of glory gone for another year. On the approach to Becher's, David Nicholson, who had been re-united with Highland Seal called, "You are well clear, kick on. Good luck." I had no intention of kicking on at that point – there was still a long way to go. Crisp flew Becher's again as if it was a hurdle. Michael O'Hehir's commentary at that point told me that my nearest rival was Red Rum, thirty lengths behind.

'The Guv'nor's words of so many years before echoed in my head: "You can't win if you don't get round." I still had eight fences to jump and one and a half miles to gallop. Crisp was still moving well with his legs flicking out in front of him and his strength giving no signs of waning. We took each of the next six jumps with precision until crossing the cinders covering the Melling Road where I felt Crisp's action change slightly.

'I said to myself, "Just two fences to go, keep hold of his head, keep him balanced." Though tiring, Crisp jumped the penultimate fence well and, having given him a breather, I drove him towards the last obstacle between us and victory. As I pushed and urged Crisp on, I caught sounds of a pursuer. The first sound I heard was the flapping of nostrils as he forced each breath out of his lungs, joined by the drumming of hoofs on the firm ground.

'Crisp popped over the last which was quite knocked about from the first time round, but he no longer had the strength to shoot away from it. Instead, his tired limbs carried his 12st burden towards the winning post at only half his previous speed. The run-in between the last fence and the line was the most agonising 494 yards that I will ever travel. My aching limbs had now given their best and every breath I snatched scalded my windpipe as if it was boiling water.

'I'd never known tiredness like it before. People think you are just sitting there; you're not. You're trying to hold the horse together and Crisp was a big, strong bugger. I was desperately trying to help but I was as far gone as he was; in fact, I was no help to him at all. I was never a very great finisher but I'm embarrassed now when I see the film of the finish, I was no use to him. Each jump takes something out of you and you feel your strength going from your fingers to start with, they begin to go a bit rubbery, and then your wrist and then right up your forearm; you have exhausted your physical depths . . .

'Crisp's action was no longer light and forward, it was now laboured and sideways as if he was drunk. The tell-tale noises got closer but so did the winning post – or did it? It almost seemed as if it was moving further away with every stride.

'With only fifteen yards to go, Crisp tensed when he felt Red Rum's presence but it was his dying effort and only lasted for a second. Two strides from the post and Red Rum's head forged past my gallant partner to snatch victory from our grasp.

'For a second I thought, "I've been beaten." But that feeling lasted literally a second. I realised immediately what I'd been through, what sensations I'd experienced; I was tingling with the deep thrills and emotions that my mind and body had experienced during those last hectic nine minutes. In fact, the time of the race was 9 mins 1.9 seconds which broke Golden Miller's 39-year-old record by no less than nineteen seconds.

'Fred Winter didn't say anything derogatory to me afterwards. It was all of three weeks later as we were driving together to a meeting when he turned and said, "You know where you lost the National." "Yes," I replied. And he said, "There's no need to talk about it then, if we both know, is there?" And that was the end of that. No recriminations. No harsh words. No inquest.

'Many trainers would have gone up the wall in a similar situation. But Fred Winter's different. He was such a good jockey that he knows a race like the

Opposite above: Becher's 1981 — some say it's like jumping off the end of the world. *Below*: Reflections on the National – clearing the water jump in 1982

The men who didn't make it: *Right*, The magnificently brave John Thorne and Spartan Missile, second left, take The Chair in 1981 before going on to finish second behind Aldaniti and, *below*, John Francome gets a ducking in Becher's after parting company with Rough and Tumble in 1982

National is a thousand decisions and if you get most of them right, that's fine.'

So where did Pitman lose the National? A wry smile spread across his battle-hardened face. 'After the last fence. Everyone thought the horse had "died" at the last fence, but he'd gone two out. I felt the action change and all the strength go out of him. He didn't jump the last very well and I thought to myself, "He's so drunk, he's almost unconscious. I've really got to wake him up."

'I took a hand off the reins to give him one and, of course, having let him down, he drifted away to the left, so then I had to pick him up and pull him back on the course to go right-handed round the elbow. Well, not only was I losing ground but momentum, too. He lost his stride even more. Now if I'd just sat still to the elbow, kept the horse balanced and then maybe given him a crack . . . There was a lot at stake and in retrospect seeing the replay, I wish I'd never hit him at all. But you make these decisions and you can't obliterate them.

'But that's the mark of Fred Winter; there's never any shouting and roaring. If you knew you'd done wrong, fine, you'd punish yourself. Fred Winter's an incredible man, a great man. If there'd been no racing, Fred Winter, like John Oaksey, would have been a great man in any other sphere . . .'

Pitman, like the great man himself and all who have ridden for Fred Winter, had a way with horses and recent years have shown that he also has a way with words for he has become a fine paddock commentator for BBC Television, a proficient writer but above all a man with a flair for just talking . . .

While Crisp remains locked in his mind forever, there are many other vivid National memories which Pitman is delighted to share.

He had six rides in all, starting with Dorimont in Foinavon's year, 1967. 'I watched the chaos at the 23rd with everyone else for I went out of it at the third fence. I always remember to this day the utter disappointment of being out of the race so soon. You cannot believe it; you sit there and you want the whole thing to be stopped and start again so you can have another crack. God only knows what it's like to fall at the first!

'You are looking forward to jumping the third, then Becher's, then the Canal Turn; you've been through it all in your mind the night before. Then, suddenly, that's it, you're out of the race and it's only just begun. And you're not going to get another chance for another year.'

A year later, Pitman was on Manifest for Winter. The form book shows that Manifest 'plodded on' to finish eleventh. Pitman sees it differently. 'Eddie Harty was Fred Winter's stable jockey at the time and he always beat me, he was always in my way, always in my hair and I could never beat him, whatever! He rode Steel Bridge for an Irish trainer and I was on Manifest and as we were going down to Valentine's second time, I recognised his colours. He was a mile in front of me but I could see he wasn't working particularly hard because he had no chance and I set off in hot pursuit. I rode as I've never ridden before or since. I was determined

The victor and the vanquished – Red Rum and Brian Fletcher (left) and the end of one of the greatest ever Nationals, with the gallant Crisp and Richard Pitman (right)

to beat him. Did I make it? You're joking . . . as soon as he saw it was me coming up behind, he let out a reef and held me off. It was a photo-finish, mind you, for tenth place!'

Pitman experienced some of the ecstasy that was to come with Crisp when he finished second in 1969 – to Harty on Highland Wedding! – on Steel Bridge, the horse which Dick Saunders had hoped to ride though Pitman insists it wasn't so. 'I knew the owner, Jimmy Drabble, and he originally bought the horse on condition that I would ride him in the National. I think what may have happened at the time was that there was a possibility I would have to ride one for Fred Winter and Dick, who went over to Ireland to ride Steel Bridge once, was approached. Mind you, no one would give a horse a better ride than Dick Saunders. Aintree is a huntsman's course and Dick is one of the finest. It's different from any other course in the world, its demands are so totally unique.'

Pitman always walked the course with Fred Winter before the National and he chuckled at the memory of their tour in 1969. 'We had a whole following of people, ear-wigging I suppose, and Jimmy Drabble, Steel Bridge's owner, came with us, too. He got whiter and whiter as we went on and the stories got bloodier and bloodier until we got to Becher's where the Guv'nor told us about falling with Sundew in 1956 when they were in second place. "We were cantering when Sundew buried me at Becher's" said Fred. "I could hear the other horses coming and the ground being depressed on either side of me and I knew I couldn't get out of the way."

'Mr Drabble was very ill at that point. He suddenly scared himself, but it does good for owners to walk round. In themselves, the fences are good and most hunting people would jump the same sort of thing and worse week in and week out but it's different when you're going flat out in the National.'

Pitman did not ride in the National again until 1972 and then, like so many jockeys before and since, picked the wrong horse. Not that it mattered in the end. John Francome was beginning to make his name in the yard but Winter gave Pitman the choice of National rides three months before the race. 'The Gov'nor said, "Make your mind up, take your pick, and stick to it." I chose Lime Street, leaving John with Cardinal Error.

'As the race grew nearer, Lime Street became less and less fancied and on the day, Cardinal Error was joint second favourite at 12–1 with Gay Trip, who had won in 1970. John decided to track me as any other young jockey might have done in his position. A young jockey with any sense will look for someone who has been round Liverpool on a fairly good ride and tuck in behind.

'What John hadn't taken into account was the fact that Lime Street wasn't the bravest horse in the world at Aintree. I first got the message when he stuck his toes in at the Melling Road as we went to look at the first fence. I knew then that I was going to be in for a hard ride. It didn't last long either. But as we almost stopped at the third, poor John was up my arse and had no chance of getting over. We baulked Cardinal Error and he refused. We came down at the fourth and that was that.'

After the excitement of Crisp, Pitman found himself on Francophile in 1974, his final ride in the National 'We had a dinner party at my house which the BBC televised and the northern boys reckoned I wouldn't even get round one circuit Martin Blackshaw gave me 3–1 and I had £50 with him and the same bet with Julian Wilson.

'When I jumped the water in nineteenth place, I took my hands off the reins, gave a salute and a laugh to signal to them that I was still there. In fact, we got as far as the 28th where Francophile refused. Like so many other horses who are tired by then, he saw that big ditch coming up and put the brakes on. But I'd won my bet . . . Jules paid me straight away but Blackshaw still owes me!'

To Pitman, like so many others the world over, there was, and still is, something extra special about the National – 'from the moment in the weighing-room where

Terry Biddlecombe would always knock the top off a bottle of champagne and share it with Josh Gifford before going out. "It makes the fences look smaller!" they used to say.

'I haven't ridden at Aintree since the Flat races stopped but in my day it was a mixed meeting and the jump jockeys were herded into the tiniest possible room. But what an atmosphere that created. There were, say, forty-two jockeys, six to eight valets, 120 saddles; you'd start to get warm, start to sweat a bit and the smell was unreal; the saddles with years of saddle soap and horse sweat! To an outsider, it was probably foul. He'd probably have walked in and said, "Oh God, this is ghastly!" But it was a smell that you recognised with that changing room at Aintree.'

The smell of the saddle soap and the roar of the crowd . . . 'It was a marvellous place to be. Before the National and after it, there's a feeling that you don't get for the rest of the year; it's a closeness of each and everyone, a bond. You are all gladiators . . .'

Gladiators with strange quirks and a whole armoury of practical jokes. Men like Graham Thorner who rode for years in the underpants he wore when winning the 1972 National for Tim Forster on Well To Do. 'He wore them until there was nothing left of them,' chuckled Pitman, 'just a bit of elastic round his legs. He had to keep them on with another pair. But there was no way he'd ride without them.

'Me? I always put on my right boot first, that was my only superstition. It was just more comfortable that way.'

And jokers like John Williams. 'He'll put a tomato in the top of someone's skull cap and when he puts it on he gets tomato all over his face, poor devil. Men become boys before the National, getting up to all sorts of silly pranks.'

Pitman has twice returned to ride Aintree since retiring from the saddle, first with John Oaksey in 1978 and then the following year with Princess Anne's husband, Captain Mark Phillips – both times for television.

'Before I went to the start with John, he said, "Look, we're both old enough and wise enough not to go and jump the third." So we went galloping over the first two chatting away to each other and as we approached the third, we pulled up and went round the fence and set off again for the cameras. I told Mark Phillips the following year what John and I had done but he said, "No, we'll jump it, that's what I'm here for!" I was on Barony Fort who had refused at the 27th two years earlier when Charlotte Brew became the first woman to ride in the National. He was a clever horse and he remembered Aintree all right and he clearly remembered the third. He started to put the brakes on but I drove him on even though he was stopping – and down we went, with me rolling over. The first person I saw was Oaksey, laughing his head off. "You silly bugger, you are a year older now but no wiser!" he roared.

Richard Pitman jumping round Aintree on Barony Fort for television in 1979, with Captain Mark Phillips on the Queen's three-day eventer, Columbus

'Mark Phillips jumped round magnificently on the Queen's horse Columbus after waiting for me to pick myself up and get going again! He proved that the fences are well within the scope of any decent horse.'

A horse like Crisp, who never returned to try again after that brave, brave attempt in 1973. 'Many people have told me it was a shame he never ran in the National again but he did get a bit of a leg after beating Red Rum at level weights at Doncaster eight months after the National. I agreed with Fred Winter when he said that Crisp had been marvellous and it would be a shame if he were to go and break down.'

Crisp has been enjoying himself hunting ever since while Pitman has been enjoying the memory of that day at Aintree in 1973. 'He was a fantastic horse with incredible guts; it was very unusual for a horse to attack those Aintree fences as he did. He was one in a million and I'm proud and fortunate to have ridden him.'

Geraldine Rees

Geraldine Rees was just nine years old when she had her first look at the Grand National fences. 'I went there with the Pony Club and we'd trot alongside Becher's and I'd look up and think to myself, "Golly, they must be mad to jump fences like that!"'

Seventeen years later, on 3 April 1982, that same Geraldine Rees, with tantalising blond hair and a figure more suited to the world of model girls than riding girls, lined up alongside thirty-seven men and one other girl, Charlotte Brew, to tackle the world's greatest steeplechase. Little more than ten minutes after the tapes went up, Geraldine crossed the line on the ten-year-old Cheers, assured of her place in history as the first woman to complete the course in the National.

Geraldine was eighth and last of the survivors but, to her, that was just like winning. 'I couldn't believe I'd actually done it; it was just fantastic,' she said as she sat and re-lived her piece of Aintree folklore.

Geraldine, born in Hampshire, the daughter of Captain James Wilson who has trained at Sollom near Preston since 1975, entered race-riding through the three-day eventing world, having represented Britain in the Junior European Championships in 1973, won at Tidworth and competed at Badminton.

'Eventing for me was purely an amateur thing but my husband Henry [they were married in 1976] and my father encouraged my race-riding and I made the most amazing start by winning with my first three rides in 1977. Frankly, I was very reluctant to give up eventing and was almost anti-racing. I just wanted to help my father to run the yard and then the whole thing took over. I was rather bewildered at first, certainly by my early success, but then I had a series of falls and decided there was more to this racing game than I'd given it credit for. That's when I really became smitten by the bug.'

By the 1981–82 season, Geraldine felt she was ready for the National though the sight of the huge fences daunted her. One run over the Mildmay course on James Ward in the 1981 Red Rum Novices' Handicap Chase was all she had to go on though she had twice ridden Twidale in hurdle races at Aintree. It was enough, however, for the atmosphere of the place to have made its impact on her.

Geraldine was set to ride Gordon's Lad when the horse went lame – just over a fortnight before the race. 'I thought that was it but my father, my husband and a group of owners said they would try and buy a horse for me to ride in the National. I was very reticent about that for it never seems to work out when people try and buy a horse for the National. Then my brother-in-law, David Rees, found Cheers and I became quite excited by the prospect. They tried, and failed, to buy the horse, so we went to the Doncaster Sales just eight days before the National to try to buy him there. Derek Beresford, one of Father's owners, bid on our behalf and went past the £5,000 we had agreed and at just over £6,000 we thought he was ours. Then the Suffolk trainer Charles Mackenzie came in at £8,000 and Cheers was gone.'

Mackenzie had bought the gelding – last of twelve finishers in the 1981 National – for his wife Sue and Susan Shally of the Burley Hill Stud near Derby, and he agreed to consider Geraldine as his National jockey. 'I spent some anxious hours waiting for Mr Mackenzie to decide on his rider before he called me on the Monday before the race to offer me the ride,' she said. And so, once more, Geraldine's tilt at the National was on.

Geraldine travelled to Newmarket on the Tuesday before Aintree in readiness to ride out the horse first thing on Wednesday. Television cameras whirred as she climbed aboard the horse who was to take her where no woman had ever been before. Back to Lancashire in the evening, across to Aintree to watch the racing on Thursday and Friday and to walk the National course for the first time in her life.

'Just as I was going out on the Thursday evening, I bumped into David Nicholson who asked what my planned tactics were for the National. "I'm going down the outside," I told him, for I'd long since made up my mind to be positive and decide exactly which way I'd go. He took me under his wing and walked the whole way round with me which was extremely kind. On the Saturday morning, however, Fred Winter came and had a chat and said, "I'll tell you the way I used to ride the course, you can listen and then make up your own mind." He said to go down the inner and with that I laughed . . . I said I hadn't really planned on doing that! But he gave me one very good piece of advice: to jump out of the gate when the tapes go up and get a good position. He told me it was important to hit the first fence right and that stuck in my mind.'

After changing for the National, Geraldine spent the last few moments rubbing resin on the seat of her breeches and inside the legs – 'for extra stickability! I was joking to a girl that I was going to get the Bostik out and she said, "Oh, no, you want to rub in resin or otherwise sit in some water and your breeches won't be so slippery." Well, I didn't fancy the water idea so my mother sent my brother Hamish off in the morning to buy some resin.'

Then, wearing her lucky pearl earrings – 'everyone said I should have something for luck and I'd always worn them racing; they were originally a present from my father to my grandmother' – Geraldine entered the parade ring, took one look at Cheers . . . and her heart sank.

'I have elastic girths on my saddle and the horse was walking round very stifled and looking tucked up. I felt there was something wrong with the horse; he looked far from happy. I asked Mr Mackenzie if the girths were too tight because they can nip a bit if they are, but he reckoned they were all right. But the horse became very worked up once I had hopped on and we were trying to sort ourselves out in numerical order for the pre-race parade. Eventually he froze completely and wouldn't move. The head lad came out and tried to encourage him to walk on but he lashed out and caught the poor chap a fearful blow at the top of a leg.

'I tried to get him to go forward but he just reared up. I was sure it was something to do with the girths and asked the boy who was leading up Cheers to let them out. As soon as he did, Cheers was OK and I relaxed a little. But not for long for Cheers froze again once the starter asked us to line up.

'My mind was in a whirl. "We are going to come under orders," I thought, "the tapes are going to go up and I'm going to be left like the Hamlet cigar advert! I can't bear it after all the hoo-ha, to be left at the start." I whipped the horse round and trotted him back towards the stands and away from the start, then turned him in and trotted up. Everyone else had sorted themselves out and I shouted at the starter, "All right, sir." He'd seen what had happened and Ron Barry was shouting to me, "Come up and join me." The tapes flew up, Ron and I went off together and we had a great run . . . I was very, very fortunate.'

And so were the punters who had taken odds of 5–1 about Geraldine getting round although husband Henry made do with £120 at 4–1. 'It was the most exciting thing of my life. I don't remember anything much until the third, we were just a huge bunch of horses. Then Coolishall, one of the early fallers, came right across me and we were nearly brought down, but I managed to avoid him and we stayed up in the front rank until Becher's.

'I admit that as we approached Becher's I thought to myself, "Oh my God, this is it," but it was not so bad because I had a clear run. I kicked Cheers and he flew over it like a bird. You feel as if your horse's legs are never going to reach the ground again but he landed safely and I told myself that the worst was over. I was lucky at The Chair because I approached it on my own; I didn't allow myself to feel frightened. I just thought, "Sit and kick, sit and kick." I caught hold of Cheers' head and pushed him forward and he just spread out over it. It was a wonderful feeling. He showed great courage all the way round.'

By the time Dick Saunders and Grittar were passing the winning post, Geraldine had long since lost touch with the actual race but she was still winning

Opposite: Geraldine Rees and Cheers take the last and go on to a place in history. 'Cheers cleared the final fence magnificently,' said Geraldine

A triumphant wave from Geraldine Rees, the first woman to complete the world's greatest steeplechase

her personal battle. 'My most vivid memory is the fantastic applause of the crowd. The first time I became properly conscious of it was at Becher's second time when the field was really strung out. I cleared it on the outside and from then on the roar was incredible. The applause all the way to the line was fantastic.'

But when the applause had died down, Geraldine suddenly found herself the target, not for praise, but abuse. Letters appeared in national newspapers accusing her of pushing Cheers too hard . . . 'It was shameful the way she forced her exhausted mount to the finishing line to satisfy her lust for glory,' said one.

Geraldine's reply is quite simple. 'Well, you can please some of the people some of the time but not all of the people all of the time. There are always going to be folk against something and while many people love racing, there are a number who think the National is cruel. I would just say this: of course, the horse was tired but he was still running and jumping well and I don't think the people who saw him falter on television on the run-in appreciated just how well he had jumped at the end. He cleared the final fences magnificently, indeed, he didn't touch a twig the whole way round.

'He jumped the last really well and then seemed to take about three strides and suddenly falter. He almost stopped, a bit like a horse refusing a fence. I thought, "My goodness, what on earth is happening, just what do I do now?" All I could do was wait because I knew the horse would tell me what to do . . . then he picked up the bridle and started to run again. I sat down and hunted him along so I was as little aggravation to him as possible.'

Geraldine admitted that she was aware of the extra pressure on her to just finish the race because the bookmakers had offered special odds about her getting round but added: 'Once I had got to the stage where I had crossed the Melling Road with only two fences to jump, then I couldn't see any reason for not carrying on. Of course, if Cheers had had something wrong with him or been distressed in any way, then I'd have pulled him up.

'I've since tried to look at it the other way and ask myself what people would have said if I'd pulled up before the last fence and, honestly, at that stage I didn't feel in any way that he wanted to stop.'

Cheers, alas, had just one more race – in the Lissington Handicap Chase at Southwell on 27 April when Geraldine pulled him up at the fourth last apparently sound enough but trainer Mackenzie said he stepped in a patch of false ground returning to the stables and severely tore the ligaments in his off foreleg. A Newmarket vet was unable to save him the following morning and Cheers was put down. 'I was terribly upset and shocked', reflected Geraldine. 'He was a tremendous horse and I will never forget how he finished in the National.' A warm, sincere tribute for a courageous horse from the girl Aintree will never forget.

Fulke Walwyn

Fulke Walwyn had just three rides in the National and completed the course only once – in 1936 when he won on Reynoldstown. It took him rather more attempts to join that select band of men who have also trained a winner but he made it in 1964 with Team Spirit.

'I've no doubt that it was easier riding the winner than training one,' said the Queen Mother's trainer as he sat in the study of Saxon House, Lambourn, surrounded by pictorial reminders of some of his countless triumphs.

'It was murder to watch for I really thought that Team Spirit would be second and I got the shakes very badly. Reynoldstown was different altogether. He had won the race the previous year when my good friend Frank Furlong rode him and we went to Aintree full of confidence.'

Few people at Aintree on Friday 27 March 1936 saw the race Fulke's way for he won in the most dramatic of circumstances as the National played its cruellest trick on the Mildmays. Lord Mildmay of Flete had bought Davy Jones for £650 for his son Anthony to ride and the tubed horse, a 100–1 outsider, looked a sound investment. Fulke, reticent to air his views at the time, now talked about it freely.

'It was only a question of which of us won as Anthony and I went well clear after Becher's second time. I made a very bad mistake at Valentine's which left me about ten lengths to make up but I got going again round the long turn to the second last, and I thought I was going the better of the two.

'We landed upsides at the second last and were very close together. Then I could hardly believe my eyes for there were his reins hanging on the ground. Anthony had his whip in his left hand and was smacking the horse across the side of the face desperately trying to keep him straight going to the last. But he had an impossible task and I actually had to take a pull and let him out. The crowd at the final fence went in all directions as the horse careered through them. It was a dreadful thing to happen to anyone and especially to someone like Anthony who, like me, so much wanted to ride a National winner.'

There was a stunned hush about Aintree as Fulke and Reynoldstown were left way, way in front but silence was golden to them. 'I just had to jump the last. It

1936, Becher's second time round. Fulke Walwyn and Reynoldstown are tracking Anthony Mildmay and Davy Jones

was a wonderful feeling coming home alone, but now that the dust has settled I honestly don't mind saying that I thought I would have won even if fate hadn't been so unkind to Davy Jones and Anthony. I didn't really know what to say to him afterwards, he was terribly upset.

'Reynoldstown was a marvellous horse – remember, he carried 12st 2 lb that day; it was a magnificent performance.' Fulke's only bad moment had been when he lost his whip on the first circuit. 'That followed a bit of a muddle at Valentine's but, as it turned out, of course, I didn't need it. If Anthony hadn't run out, however, I probably would have done.'

Thirty-eight years later and Fulke lost his hat as Team Spirit and Willie Robinson held off Purple Silk and John Kenneally by a heart-thumping half a length. 'Yes, I threw my hat in the air as they passed the post although from our position in Lord Derby's box I wasn't absolutely sure we'd won. And it wasn't until after the following race that a kind chap came up to me and handed back my hat!'

Fulke derived tremendous pleasure from the success of Team Spirit since he had twice been second with horses he trained for Dorothy Paget – Legal Joy in 1952 and Mont Tremblant the following year. Team Spirit had been trained originally in Ireland by Dan Moore and arrived at Lambourn after four unsuccessful attempts at the National. This was just six months before the 1963

Fulke Walwyn gets that winning feeling as, *opposite*, he is led in on Reynoldstown after storming home in 1936, and, *above*, as Team Spirit, avoiding the riderless Lizawake, is driven up by Willie Robinson to head Purple Silk and John Kenneally (rails) in 1964, enabling Walwyn to join that select band of men who have both ridden and trained a National winner

race in which he finished fourth to Ayala after Fulke had sent him out to win the Grand Sefton at Aintree.

Dan's wife Joanie schooled and rode out the little horse who had been bought for 350 guineas with the hunting field in mind until, as a four-year-old, he was put in a gallop with older horses being prepared for point-to-points in Meath country. To everyone's amazement, Team Spirit galloped clear. Dan passed him on to one of his patrons, Doreen Brand and the horse was then sold for £4,000 to three Americans – Ron Woodard, Jack Goodman and Gamble North.

Team Spirit, who fell at Becher's second time round in 1960 and finished ninth in 1961, fell at the 19th in 1962 before moving to Fulke on Dan's advice. But 1964 was very much Team Spirit's year. He was third approaching the stands on the first circuit and then jumped clear of the fallers at The Chair before taking the water splendidly. He stayed in third place some way behind the leaders, Peacetown and Out and About, until the Canal Turn where he fell back a few places, appearing to have had enough.

Team Spirit, however, twelve years old by now, was nothing if not tough and

Right: Minutes after victory, American owners Ron Woodard, Jack Goodman and Gamble North gather round Team Spirit

Below: The day after victory: the Lambourn locals turn out to welcome Team Spirit and Fulke Walwyn

Right : The King of Aintree, Red Rum, with his trainer, Ginger McCain.

Below: Dick Saunders, the oldest winning rider of the National, talks the race through with David Coleman of BBC Television

Above: A collector's item – the Aynsley Plate, created for the Grand National Appeal launched in November 1982. Long Live the National! *Right*: At the end of the supreme test for one man and his horse there is a unique sense of achievement – and for the winning owner, this magnificent Grand National Aynsley Trophy

after getting his second wind, he regained third place as they came back on to the racecourse. There he stayed until after the last with Fulke's heart thumping. 'Purple Silk, who had been waiting on Peacetown, hit the front after the last and took the inside track home. It was a desperate battle to the line but Willie rode Team Spirit splendidly and took the lead in the last fifty yards, but it was oh so close and my nerves could hardly stand it!' Fulke's wife, Cath, such an important member of the Saxon House team, was emotionally drained, too.

The celebrations at The Adelphi went on long into the early hours and some sleepers complained of being woken at 5 am on Sunday to a reverberating rendering of 'Chicago, Chicago'. Fulke – fellow revellers of days gone by will tell you he was a legend in his own party-time! – chuckled at the memory. 'Yes, we had a good party; after all, we'd won the National!'

Even now, after gracing the National Hunt scene for five decades with courage and skill, warmth and humour, the great race remains extra special to Fulke. 'It is impossible to imagine life without the National; it means so much to so many sportsmen.'

Fred Winter

Fred Winter's heart sank when he first set eyes on the eleven-year-old bay gelding Kilmore, his ride for the 1961 Grand National. He had just won the Champion Hurdle on Eborneezer for his guv'nor Ryan Price, and Kilmore, who had been bought for £3,000 by three show business friends, Nat Cohen, Ben Rosenfeld and Pinky Taylor, was about to run in the following race, the Kim Muir Memorial Challenge Cup.

Winter grabbed his overcoat and binoculars from his valet, Dave Stalker, and went down to the paddock to take a look at Kilmore. 'He looked horrible,' recalled Winter, 'and I felt worse still as I watched him trail round to finish sixth behind Nicolaus Silver. I went up to Ryan afterwards and said, "Oh, Ryan, what have you done to me?"'

Eleven days later – on Sunday 19 March – Winter drove to Lingfield Park to school Kilmore over eight fences in company with two other horses. 'He fell at the first ditch and I had to run alongside to catch him, but after that we jumped the two up the hill and three in the straight and the way he pinged the last lifted my spirits no end. He'd also met the last fence but one all wrong; I left him alone and Kilmore took one more very quick stride and flew the fence so I knew, too, that he had some brains.'

The National that year featured two Russian horses for the first time, and previous winners Merryman II and Mr What, as well as Wyndburgh who had twice been second and Team Spirit, who was to win in 1964. The race was won by Nicolaus Silver, who had won the Kim Muir, but Kilmore ran magnificently finishing fifth, leaving Winter to observe: 'Kilmore never put a foot wrong but I think I made too much use of him.'

Winter relished the prospect of riding Kilmore at Aintree again the following year, a year he used to get to know inside out the horse who was to provide him with his greatest National memory.

'Kilmore started the 1961–62 season by carrying 11st 11lb into second place behind John O'Groats in the 3-mile Whitelaw Gold Cup at Folkestone on 25 September before returning to Aintree for the Becher Chase over 2 miles 5

Fred Winter's first taste of National triumph as he takes the last on Sundew in 1957

furlongs on 3 November. Disaster! We fell at the 6th, and we ended up on the floor again at Lingfield in the Sussex Handicap Chase on 21 March. In between, however, Josh Gifford had ridden Kilmore unplaced in the Hennessy Gold Cup and I had finished fifth on him in the Mildmay Memorial Chase at Sandown.

'To make sure he stayed the 4½ miles at Liverpool, I reckoned that I needed to settle him down and not make so much use of him as I had in the previous National. So at Lingfield, I put this into practice, dropping him out early on. He settled well and was jumping brilliantly. Then, as we went into the 13th, an open ditch about a mile and a quarter out in the 3-mile race, I began to ask him to quicken and get into the race with a chance. I gave him a kick going into the jump and the next moment we were on the floor. It had been just the same when we fell in the Becher Chase at Liverpool and, with hindsight, I realise how lucky I was to fall again at Lingfield.

'I knew then, that once I had him settled and popping his fences, I could not suddenly ask him to quicken. I would have to sit and suffer at Aintree. To wait and wait and wait . . . and that is exactly what I did.

'National Day itself was a shocker. The race was run in appalling conditions; the heavy rain and earlier frosts reduced the going to a mudpatch, so unusual for Aintree. The previous year's winner, Nicolaus Silver, and Merryman II who had won in 1960, were totally unsuited by the going though the necessary slower pace of the race was undoubtedly responsible for the fact that seventeen of the thirty-two runners completed the course.

'Kilmore and I were so far behind going past the stands and out into the country on the second circuit that I remember calling out to John Oaksey, who was just in front of me on Taxidermist, "John, please give me some room." "Good God," replied John, "I didn't think there was anybody behind me!"

'Frenchman's Cove, the 7–1 favourite, was going well until he was brought down at the 19th, but as we turned for home for the second time, I had Kilmore in sixth place while the Irish outsiders Gay Navarree and Fredith's Son disputed the lead with Mr What, Nicolaus Silver and Wyndburgh close behind. I did not let Kilmore go until the last fence but one, and then there was no looking back. We took the lead approaching the last and Kilmore ran on strongly to win by ten lengths and the same from Wyndburgh and Mr What.

'I think winning on Kilmore that day was the most satisfying win I ever had in my life. We had worked twelve months for that victory and it was great to achieve our objective; it was wonderful, too, to give Ryan Price his first National winner.'

Kilmore's triumph is one of four reasons why Winter became known as Mr Grand National – he also rode Sundew to victory in 1957 and won with Jay Trump (1965) and Anglo (1966) in his first two years as a trainer. What to him, then, makes the National so different from other races?

'You get keyed up for other big races like the Gold Cup and Champion Hurdle,

Victory number two coming up for Fred Winter as he leads over the last on Kilmore in 1962 from, left to right, Mr What and J. Lehane (third), Gay Navarree and A. Cameron (fourth) and Wyndburgh and T. Barnes (second)

of course, but the build-up to the National is something else. You start possibly a month or more before, thinking about it, dreaming about it. With Kilmore, the build-up lasted a year. It is the honour of winning this race that means so much.'

What about the fences, are they really more terrifying than others elsewhere? 'They are more formidable. Terrifying doesn't seem the right word, but they certainly take more jumping than fences on other courses. I never got tired of riding round Aintree. In fact, the more you do it, the more you enjoy it because you become the master of it.'

Winter certainly became the master and his theory on riding in the National is required reading for any aspiring Aintree jockey. 'I favoured sticking to the inside all the way and giving my horse every possible chance by not chasing the leaders.

Fred Winter and Kilmore being led in after the 1962 triumph. 'The most satisfying win of my life,' recalled Winter

I'll never forget Pat Taaffe telling me what Dan Moore told him. This was that you hunt round the first two miles and then think about being a jockey. This is true and if you watched Pat going to a fence in the National, you would see him pulling the horse back. It was really quite remarkable. You could almost hear him saying, "Steady, steady," as he pulled the horse right back on to his hocks so that he got exactly the right trajectory.'

And what about the horse, what does Winter look for in a National horse? 'He needs to be courageous and a good jumper. He should be clever, rather than bold – a thinker. Any normal animal can jump the jumps but only the brainy ones can win the race.' A horse, indeed, like Kilmore – though if horses could talk, we fancy he would have agreed that a jockey like Fred Winter also had something to

Victory number three for Fred Winter – in his first attempt as a trainer. Owner Mary Stephenson looks admiringly at Jay Trump after the 1965 National

do with conquering the National. Together they took part in four successive Nationals, a magnificent partnership which was not separated until the 21st fence in the 1964 race. By then, they had successfully negotiated 110 fences over more than fifteen miles round Aintree, a magnificent record.

Kilmore lived in happy retirement with Ryan Price at Findon until dying in 1981 at the age of thirty-one.

The Yankee Double

Tommy Smith and Charlie Fenwick, a pair of American amateur riders, each had a horse which had twice won the Maryland Hunt Cup, equivalent in honour to the Grand National. They each nurtured a dream of bringing that horse to England and winning the National; they each showed an obsessive, single-mindedness which enabled them to conquer Aintree.

Smith was twenty-six when he arrived at Lambourn with his new bride Frances, and the bay gelding Jay Trump in July 1964. He spent the next six months eating, sleeping, drinking the National in the care of Fred Winter and on 27 March 1965 Smith became the first American rider to win the race, the first amateur for nineteen years while Jay Trump was the first American horse to triumph for twenty-seven years. 'What a race. I'd never seen anything like it,' recalled Smith.

Fenwick was thirty when he arrived in Oxfordshire in November 1978 with his wife Ann to join the pony-sized chestnut Ben Nevis, who had been flown over four months earlier. He spent the next four months in the care of Tim Forster eating, sleeping, drinking the National – but on 31 March 1979 Fenwick and Ben Nevis became just another National statistic as they were brought down by a loose horse at The Chair. 'It was a great thrill up until then, but at The Chair I had to jump the ditch, the fence and another horse. I couldn't manage all three,' said Fenwick.

That experience had done nothing to get the National out of Fenwick's system – an enthusiasm fuelled by his family's link with that very same Tommy Smith; Tommy's wife, Frances, is a first cousin of Charlie's wife, Ann.

Fenwick continued to think of little else but winning the National though business commitments in Baltimore, where he is a banker, prevented him from being anything other than a commuter-jockey. And, incredibly, on 29 March 1980, his dream, too, came true as he finished twenty lengths clear of John Francome and Rough and Tumble. 'I've never known anything like competing against twenty-nine of the top jockeys in the world. It was a real ordeal.'

Now back in the States, Tommy Smith and Charlie Fenwick love nothing more than telling and re-telling the story of the day they won the world's greatest steeplechase . . .

Smith is the third generation of amateur steeplechase riders whose grandfather Harry Worcester Smith and father Crompton never tired of discussing Aintree and the Grand National. Neither had been able to ride in the race; Tommy vowed he would – and that he would win! An illustrated map of the Grand National course hung over the fireplace at Featherbed Farm in the middle of the Virginia foxhunting country where the Smith family lived.

By the time he came to England, he was unashamedly consumed with one thing and one thing only – winning the National. His attention to detail was amazing. With the invaluable help of his younger sister Kitty, Tommy worked out Jay Trump's diet so that it precisely matched the American diet the horse had been used to before flying to England.

Smith could hardly have had a better tutor than Fred Winter who resolved 'to teach him race-riding in England which is a very different thing from race-riding in the States'. Winter recalled: 'Tommy was clearly such a good rider that we hardly had to change his style or ways at all. He did, like many Americans, ride on his toes rather than on the ball of the foot, but as he had been so successful riding that way, I felt he was best left alone even though I myself don't particularly like that method.'

All went well. Jay Trump qualified to be handicapped for the National by winning the Autumn Trial at Sandown on 21 October 1964 and Smith demonstrated to Winter for the first time how uncannily he could carry out the trainer's instructions. Winter said: 'It was almost as if I had ridden the race myself.' It was a demonstration that was to be repeated at Aintree.

There was, however, an anxious ten days immediately prior to the big day. One by one, Winter's horses went down with the cough and it was decided to move Jay Trump into total isolation. He was moved to Dyer's Yard across from Kapal Cottage where Tommy and Frances were living. Tommy hardly left Jay Trump's side, only handing over to a security guard at seven o'clock each night. Smith did everything for the horse: he cared for him like a child, mucking out, dressing, feeding, exercising him. 'I hadn't come all that way and spent all those weeks of preparation for my dream to be ruined then,' he said.

Jay Trump evidently missed the hustle and bustle of everyday life at Uplands but Tommy talked with him unceasingly – teasing and playing with him – during those final long ten days before the National. But by the time the big day arrived, Tommy was showing signs of strain. He had lost weight, had not been able to sleep and his sinuses had flared up. The bookmakers, who in February had made Jay Trump 12–1 favourite for the National, pushed out his price to 25–1.

When Jay Trump and forty-six opponents faced the starter, he was still priced

The best of friends – Tommy Smith
and Jay Trump

at 100–6, but the bookmakers had underestimated Tommy Smith. He listened intently as Winter gave the final orders: 'Ride the race the way Jay Trump wants it to be ridden, not the way everybody else is riding. Go at a pace and take up a position most advantageous to him; don't go too fast too soon, stay out of danger – and stay on the inside.'

Smith did it so perfectly that Winter said later: 'My overwhelming memory is the uncanny way Tommy rode the race. It was a virtual replica of my successful ride on Kilmore in 1962; a dream race if ever I saw one . . .'

Tommy Smith's dream came true. 'I must admit that when I first saw the fences I was horrified, just horrified. They were truly much bigger in real life than I had imagined and by the time of the race itself, the pressure had become intense. Jay Trump's owner, Mrs Mary Stephenson, had flown over from Ohio and my mother, Margot, was at Aintree, too. Bobby Fenwick, one of Jay Trump's former trainers, also flew over.' Fenwick in fact collected £4000 from the bookies!

'Sure, I was scared before the start. But I was always scared. We had watched films of the great race back home time after time and knew it to be the greatest steeplechase in the world. I had always wanted to ride in it as long as I could remember. Jay Trump was insured for $50,000 in case anything happened to him

Tommy Smith, in a perfect position throughout, and Jay Trump (5) track the favourite Freddie and Pat McCarron after landing over Valentine's

in the race, but I'd never fallen off him and I didn't intend to make it a first time at Aintree.'

Jay Trump and Tommy Smith never looked like parting company and only Freddie, the 7–2 favourite and Pat McCarron, stood between them and victory as they came over the Melling Road and on to the racecourse for the final time. They jumped the second last with barely an inch between them, then Jay Trump opened up a tiny gap by the last and seemed sure to win as he set off on that agonising run-in. But McCarron drove Freddie on and the horses were locked together in the last 200 yards. Tommy Smith kept his nerve, Jay Trump kept going and they won by three-quarters of a length.

Smith will never forget the race: 'I had been told to get to the inside and stay there, and the horses were going a good gallop so I pulled back to the inside. I was in the first fifteen going to the Canal Turn where I had a good jump landing about third. I didn't want to be there that soon so I "took back". At the third fence after that a horse fell in front of me and my horse landed on the rider. My heart missed a beat, and we lost a lot of ground. Everyone seemed to pick up down to The Chair and I went back to about twelfth. I gradually recovered ground, fence by fence, and at the Canal Turn I had another super jump, taking me into second. Then a couple of horses went past me again and went on after Freddie. I decided I had better stay with Freddie, and I did.'

Tommy Smith and the Great American Dream had come true – just as it was to

The moment Tommy Smith had dreamed about – he passes the post first on Jay Trump with Freddie in second place

come true for Charlie Fenwick fifteen years later. In many ways, Fenwick's triumph at the second attempt was even more incredible for when he set out with Ben Nevis at Aintree on 29 March 1980, he was entitled to have been suffering from jet-lag after flying over from the States only forty-eight hours earlier.

And Ben Nevis? When he first began his career in England in 1974 he was nothing more than a moderate point-to-pointer about which *Hunter Chasers and Point-to-Pointers* of 1975 noted dryly: 'Did well to win on his third appearance [he had fallen in his first two]. May turn out like his half-brother Gay Truant – speedy, a bad jumper and only able to last a bare three miles . . .' He went to the States and was a revelation under Fenwick, never being beaten.

When he arrived at Letcombe Bassett in 1978 to be trained by Tim Forster, he had the reputation still of being a desperate ride. But Fenwick is quick to defend his horse. 'He wasn't really a runaway, he just loved his racing. I admit, however, he was not a piece of cake. He was a very strong horse and one which liked firm ground; he hated really heavy ground.'

Forster recalled: 'When Ben Nevis first came to me from America, I thought he was the smallest and lightest animal ever to set foot in my yard. He didn't even look a half-brother to a racehorse but he obviously had great courage.'

All the planning, all the sleepless nights were wasted in a flash when Charlie and Ben came a cropper at The Chair in 1979 but Fenwick was not finished with the National. Forster had to plan races for Ben Nevis during the following season around Fenwick's availability – he flew to England seven times on cheap standby flights to ride his horse.

'There were many difficulties involved in training Ben Nevis,' said Forster. 'I had been told he needed rock-hard ground to run on and we often didn't get it. I took him to Doncaster just over a month before the National for the High Melton Handicap Chase and the going was desperately heavy. We really shouldn't have run but Charlie came over specially and I just couldn't pull out the horse and say, "We're going home, it's raining."'

Ben Nevis trailed in third that day, beaten over thirty lengths, and always seemed to be struggling throughout the final circuit. Then, amazingly, just like Jay Trump, he was the centre of a coughing scare days before Aintree. 'Ben Nevis coughed fifteen times on the Tuesday before the National,' recalled Fenwick, 'but Tim Forster didn't dare tell me!'

Looking back, Forster readily admitted his worries. 'In normal circumstances, I doubt whether I would have run Ben Nevis. But the whole shooting match was on its way over from America and after satisfying myself that the horse was all right, we had nothing to lose in running. Frankly, I didn't fancy Ben Nevis one bit. Nobody could have made me have a shilling on him. I did fancy him in 1979 but then look what happened!'

National Day brought the one thing Fenwick did not want – desperate going,

All the planning, all the sleepless nights were wasted in a flash as Charlie Fenwick and Ben Nevis came a cropper at The Chair in 1979

Opposite: Over! Charlie Fenwick and Ben Nevis make for home after taking the final fence well clear in 1980

the most gruelling conditions anyone could remember. And from thirty starters only four finished. Fenwick thrust Ben Nevis – a 40–1 outsider this time after being a 14–1 chance in 1979 – ahead at Becher's second time round when the leader Delmoss crashed. From that moment on, nothing came near him until he crossed the finishing line, triumphant.

'He gave me a fantastic ride,' said Fenwick, 'and yet how he hated the mud! Amazing! He never went better, he was strong the whole way and just kept galloping on. I never really got to the bottom of him. It was no test of speed, only of stamina. I think he remembered The Chair from the previous year for we struggled a bit at that fence, but it's a struggle for every horse, I think. Even so, he jumped it fine and as for Becher's, well, he was magnificent there both times.

'He went off the bit at the cross fence and I just slapped him and knew there was still a lot left; he never seemed to get tired. I was waiting for John Francome to come up beside me on Rough and Tumble but he never arrived. I could not believe it as we crossed the Melling Road. He took a hold of his bit and I knew

then that John would have to really work to catch us. Poor John, he had schooled Ben over hurdles after racing at Newbury the previous Saturday!

'I was a very lucky man because so much was due to the way Ben and I were "programmed" by Captain Forster and his stable jockey Graham Thorner, who had won on Well To Do in 1972. I may not have been the most stylish rider out there that day, but at least I was fit. And, thank God, so was the horse. It is the toughest competition I have ever been involved in but I prepared myself well back home by riding out every day and playing a lot of squash so I was sure I could last the 4½ miles.

'The horse's years of jumping solid, upright timber fences in Maryland certainly stood him in good stead and despite what happened in 1979, I was always confident he could jump round Aintree. I was more worried about the drops on the landing side than the height of the fences. I happened to be a passenger on a horse that was the best on the day.'

Forster, for one, would not go along with that for he said: 'Charlie's performance was amazing. Surely, the most remarkable ever. People talk about jet-lag – there can't be any such thing as far as Charlie is concerned.'

The only sad note for Fenwick was the absence from Aintree of his father-in-law, the horse's owner, Redmond C. Stewart, who had bought Ben Nevis as a seven-year-old in 1974 over the dinner table in Yorkshire after a shooting party. He was unable to travel because of his wife's ill health.

But Charlie more than made up for the disappointment of his grandfather, whose horse Billy Barton rose at the last in the lead alongside Tipperary Tim in the 1928 National only to capsize at the fence. He was remounted to finish second to the 100–1 winner in a forty-two horse field in which they were the only two to complete.

Everything came up roses for Charlie Fenwick at Aintree in 1980 just as it had for Tommy Smith, fifteen years earlier. But the last word must go to Redmond C. Stewart, who said: 'The whole of foxhunting America would rather win your Grand National than any other race.'

Dick Saunders

Dick Saunders, forty-eight-year-old Northamptonshire farmer who had never even seen a Grand National live, never mind ride in one, came, saw and conquered the race at the first time of asking on 3 April 1982 and then calmly announced: 'That's it, I'll never race-ride again.'

What a way to go . . . the first member of the Jockey Club ever to ride the winner; the oldest winning rider since Tommy Pickernell triumphed on Pathfinder in 1875 at the tender age of forty-one; along with Lord Manners, who won on Seaman in 1882, he was one of only two men to ride once in the race and win it.

Who, we had asked ourselves, could possibly follow the romance of the previous year surrounding the triumph of Bob Champion and Aldaniti? In Dick Saunders and his nine-year-old partner, Grittar, we had the perfect combination – the true amateur, a real sportsman in every sense of the word and a horse, bred and trained in Leicestershire by his sixty-seven-year-old owner, Frank Gilman.

Saunders reacted just as his best friends knew he would – with calm, modesty, embarrassment almost, as the cheers rang out for him. 'I did nothing. Grittar did it all. He jumped superbly and was never under pressure.' That boyish smile, laughing blue eyes, his impish sense of fun . . .

'Have you seen the video of the race? You can see me just approaching the 23rd and there's John Francome going head first into Becher's after parting with Rough and Tumble . . . I think that's hilarious. Dear old John, he's such a brilliant rider and a lovely chap . . .' You are almost tempted to think that the sight of the champion jockey joining the ghost of Captain Becher is Dick's greatest National memory!

It is essential to understand Saunders' approach to life to appreciate how he was able to react so coolly to everything. It was that very level-headed attitude which made him a winner – make no mistake, a proud, proud winner – of the world's greatest steeplechase. He starved himself of riding in his twenties while he built his farm into a 3000-acre operation over the rolling Northamptonshire grasslands; he did not ride his first winner under National Hunt rules until 1966

It's looking rough for John Francome as he drops into Becher's after parting company with Rough and Tumble in 1982

though more than a hundred followed along with over a hundred in point-to-points.

'I rode probably more winners against professionals than amateurs,' said Saunders, 'and my attitude to racing was to go out there and do the best possible for the horse and for the owner.' He was continually pestered before Aintree with the same question: Are you riding just because you want to ride in the National? Dick's answer was always the same. 'Look, I'm going out there the same as any professional. That is the way my mind works. I'm there to win.' Then, almost apologetically, he corrected himself . . . 'not that I ever thought I'd win the National.'

Saunders admitted that a ride in the National was never an all-consuming ambition. 'I only ever wanted to ride in the race if I could be on a horse that I thought was entitled to be there. Frankly, I never thought I'd have the opportunity because nearly all the horses with the weight I could do were in large stables with retained jockeys.

'I would, however, have ridden Steel Bridge in the 1969 race – but was jocked off! I went over to Ireland and won on the horse at Punchestown. He was being trained by Barbara Lockhart-Smith for the National and she and the owner asked me what weight I would carry. At that time, I had reduced my riding weight to 10st 7lb which meant he would be carrying 7lb overweight. They totally accepted that and the horse came over from Ireland. I put up 8lb overweight and was unplaced at Wye on 3 March before Stan Mellor won on him at Lingfield eighteen days later carrying 10st.

'They all began to get a bit excited and a few days before Aintree decided that the horse should carry his alloted 10st. I told Barbara, "If that's what you want, it's up to you but don't ever ask me to ride another horse for you again." They engaged Richard Pitman, and Steel Bridge, who started at 33–1, finished second. It was disappointing for me, of course, but Dick probably gave him a better ride than I would have done; he may not have been second with me, who knows.'

While Steel Bridge was finishing twelve lengths behind Toby Balding's Highland Wedding, Saunders forgot his disappointment and went off to a point-to-point – and rode a winner! 'That's where I went every Grand National Day – enjoying myself point-to-pointing. Certainly, I always watched the race on television in the dressing-room but that's the closest I'd been until Grittar came along . . .'

Saunders was happy enough with a few rides in the Foxhunters on the opening day of the Liverpool meeting – and chuckled at the memory of his second ride on Lady Kin in 1970. 'I fell at Becher's, remounted, fell again at the 14th but remounted once more and managed to finish second a distance behind Andrew Wates and Lismateige. Now, there's a coincidence: Andrew trained Hard Outlook who was second to Grittar in the National and Anthony Webber, who rode Hard Outlook that day, had his first ride under rules on Lady Kin for us. And guess who pulled up next to us in the car park on National Day? Yes, Andrew Wates! That would have been enough for many people to have had a coincidence bet, wouldn't it?'

Betting is one item not on Dick's agenda though as the 1982 National drew nearer, more and more good judges began to make Grittar and his grey-haired amateur partner a sound investment for the race. They had, after all, won the Foxhunters over one circuit of the National course in 1981 by an impressive twenty lengths from Sydney Quin.

'That was the key to everything,' observed Saunders. 'There is no doubt that the fences are awe-inspiring, though we jump big drop fences hunting so we're used to that sort of thing. But it's the ditches really that make Aintree so different, particularly at The Chair. I was slightly worried about that fence in the Foxhunters because Grittar is a horse who is fairly intelligent and I reckoned that if we got it wrong at The Chair, we might have problems. I told Frank Gilman at the time, "I think he'll jump round all right, he has the ability to get round but he does think and I must get it right at that fence. If we get it right there, we'll win!"

'It's a narrow but high and wide fence with flimsy wings and I felt sure it would worry Grittar if we got in a mess there. I felt he wouldn't jump the rest of the course well and Aintree is all about jumping . . .'

Saunders need not have worried. Grittar flew The Chair and apart from a hiccup at Becher's where Paul Webber – 'those Webbers again!' – and Sydney Quin came across Grittar – 'if I hadn't been there, he'd have fallen for I propped him up!' – everything went perfectly. It was, without doubt, an impressive Grand National trial for the real thing in 1982.

Saunders went back to his farm. Those who know no better began touting for Gilman to replace the amateur pilot with a top professional and the noises became louder when Francome rode Grittar into second place in the Whitbread Trial Handicap Chase at Ascot on 10 February – he rode because Saunders could not do the weight of 10st 3lb although Francome himself put up 5lb overweight.

Shades of 1969 and Steel Bridge! 'Oh, no,' said Saunders. 'There was never any question that I wouldn't ride Grittar though I did tell Frank that I would quite understand if he wanted to get the best professional he could for the horse. But Frank has been very, very loyal to me and there was never any argument whatsoever. Grittar's weight for the National, 11st 5lb, didn't present a problem and any weight difficulties were the only circumstances, I think, under which Frank might have hesitated.

'After all, I knew the horse well. I'd ridden him in his first point-to-point as a six-year-old and I remember Frank saying to me in the paddock then, "This is a racehorse, boy!" Always called me "boy". He was right, of course. Grittar is an outstanding horse.'

Dick's daughter, Caroline, rode Grittar as a seven-year-old, twice winning on him but – 'I was shooting with Frank one day in the autumn of 1980 when he said, "I think you'd better ride the old horse this season, boy. Caroline has had a great year but maybe he needs stronger riding now." At the time, I'd been wondering whether to carry on riding after sticking some ribs through a lung but that was that. Frank said I'd ride, so I rode!'

Saunders and Grittar trod the path taken the previous year by his late, great friend John Thorne and Spartan Missile and ran in the Gold Cup at Cheltenham before the National. Like Thorne and Spartan Missile, they put up a splendid performance, running on to be sixth. The sixteen days between that race and Aintree tested even Saunders' Corinthian calm.

'The publicity build-up did begin to get at me. Everybody seemed to hone in on Grittar and me, and I reckon I spent the equivalent of two days giving interviews before the race . . . and I still had my farm to run! The pressures on me were enormous, everyone seemed to be talking about Grittar and me. Normally when that happens, the whole thing is an anti-climax and you fall at the first!'

Saunders decided therefore to drive to Liverpool on the opening day of the National meeting with his wife Pam – 'so I could walk the course on my own in peace and quiet, and that is exactly what I did. I went quietly round by myself, just planning what I would do if I had the opportunity. I decided where I'd be at each fence, particularly on the second circuit and how I would jump them.'

He stayed to watch the Foxhunters and then drove back to Northamptonshire. 'There was work to do on the Friday and the men to be paid. I didn't change my routine at all; a glass of wine in the evening and early to bed. We were up at seven o'clock on Saturday morning and drove to Aintree on our own because Caroline had to ride in a point-to-point.

'We were very particular about one thing, however. Both Pam and I wore exactly the same clothes we had on the previous year when we went to Liverpool for the Foxhunters. I am a little superstitious like that.'

Saunders revelled in the camaraderie of the weighing-room on National Day. 'What a wonderful atmosphere: everyone wishing each other luck; marvellous. I loved it.' And then the walk through the crowds and into the paddock and more nerve-wracking moments before getting up on Grittar and riding into history. What were Frank Gilman's instructions? 'Oh, we didn't really discuss the race. There were no instructions; he told me an amusing story instead! I don't know whether that was to relax me or what.'

By the time the tapes went up, Grittar was the 7–1 favourite in a field of thirty-nine.

'I jumped off near the inner since I'd decided that I'd go for the tight inside. At first I used to go down the middle or outer at Aintree and I think it took me about four rides to get to know the course and decide that the best place to keep out of

trouble is straight along the inside. I've always been an inside man ever since I took racing fairly seriously; either you are or you aren't. I think you are less likely to get your bad jumpers up the inside and the loose horses can get out there at Aintree whereas it's not so easy for them to get out on the outside.

'And, apart from anything else, it's the shortest way! I remember someone once telling me it's 800 yards shorter round the inside over two circuits of the National course. I can't believe it's as much as that, but it must be a long, long way because it's a very wide course.

'Bill Smith on Delmoss was on the inside, too, and he went away smartly. That was fine for it more or less left me the running rail. By the time I'd jumped the first, I'd certainly got the inside so I was always in the position I wanted.'

There were ten casualties at the first fence including Aldaniti and Bob Champion while the much-fancied top weight Royal Mail departed at Becher's. Grittar and Saunders flipped over The Chair in third place and, by Becher's second time around, found themselves in front.

'Everything was working out incredibly well, just as I'd planned on that Thursday morning walk. I'd never thought I'd really be able to put it all into practice in the actual race with so many runners. I was slightly worried on a couple of occasions by loose horses going off the course because Grittar was a bit busy watching them and not concentrating going into a fence. I had to say, "Come here and concentrate."

'I was in front sooner than I would have wished but the horse was running so

Brough Scott congratulates Dick Saunders at an historic moment: Saunders was the first member of the Jockey Club ever to ride the National winner; at forty-eight he was the oldest winning rider; with Lord Manners, who won on Seaman in 1882, he was one of only two men to ride just once in the race and win it

well, it was pointless not going on. Apart from the Canal Turn where the horse was just running a bit too free, it all went according to plan. I'd seen a long stride at the Canal Turn some way out and I reckoned that if I was going to angle him it was likely to unbalance him – and the last thing you want to do over those fences is to unbalance your horse. It's better to go a few yards further. It did mean he jumped the fence a bit straight and landed a long way out which meant I lost a bit of ground but he came round on an even keel and, of course, it didn't matter since we were in front because all the others followed. It's when you're behind that you want to get every inch of ground that you can there, because you can be taken so wide so easily; they all follow the leading horse and very few try to come up the inside on you.'

Standing there at the Canal Turn was one man who admired and envied Saunders more than most – the Prince of Wales, who attended the National with the Princess of Wales for the first time. The Prince later wrote a four-page letter of congratulation to Saunders – 'that was a bit extra, wasn't it' – who treasured that and a telegram from the Queen Mother among the scores of good wishes.

After the Canal Turn, there were just two more fences and that long run-in between Saunders and victory; they never looked like faltering. 'I never looked round and apart from Grittar's breathing, I didn't hear a sound. I just kept kicking for home. If you've done as much race-riding as me, you're only concentrating on one thing and that's winning.

Perfect partners – Frank Gilman, breeder, owner and trainer of Grittar, with Dick Saunders, a true amateur and a real sportsman

'As I pulled up, the first person to come over and congratulate me was Bob Champion. I hadn't realised he'd gone at the first, of course. He'd run back to watch the race on the big screen they had at Aintree for the first time. Before the race, he'd been ribbing me about beating us and I'd said, "All right, we'll make it a dead heat." Not that I ever really expected to win . . .'

There were just eight finishers in all, with Richard Hoare performing wonders to finish third on Loving Words after being brought down four fences from home. Richard vaulted back on the grey with the others gone, apparently beyond recall. Four horses were at least 100 yards ahead as he galloped across the Melling Road. But he clawed back enough up that run-in to deny Delmoss and Bill Smith of third place on the line.

Opposite: If only horses could talk, what a tale they'd tell: Aldaniti and Kilmore, two great Aintree heroes

Grittar was the first outright favourite to win since Merryman II in 1960. 'The reaction was unbelievable,' said Saunders. 'I had messages and telegrams from all manner of people, many of whom I'd never met in my life; one came from a girl in Australia who I'd known as a teenager in Northamptonshire.'

Dick's son, Toby, Caroline's twin, watched the race in Australia where he was working at the time. 'I rang him on the Sunday morning; he was very excited by it all.'

Once the interviews were over, Saunders was back on the motorway heading for home. 'Saturday was the closing day for entries for our point-to-point the following week so I had to make sure everything was okay.'

Caroline was there to greet Dick with, alas, a sad tale to tell. She had won her opening race at the Grafton Point-to-Point, watched the National on television and then gone out to ride a Hotfoot mare that had never run before. 'The horse had a lot of ability, but fell and broke its neck; that's the ups and downs of racing, you see, it's a great leveller.'

Dick Saunders has always had his feet firmly on the ground. How appropriate then that he should win at a time when the National was once more under threat and in an age where sportsmanship often counts for so little. 'To me, the National is the one great race we have within steeplechasing; world-wide it means far more than any race. It has unbelievable appeal. We've lost so much in this country, it would be very sad to lose the National.'

And so say all of us . . . Long Live the National!

Appendix of Grand National Winners 1839-1982

Year	Winner	Owner	Trainer	Rider	Age	Wts. st. lbs.	Time min. sec.	S.P.	No. of Strs.
1839	LOTTERY	Mr. Elmore	Dockeray	J. Mason		12 0	14 52	5-1	17
1840	JERRY	Mr. Elmore		B. Bretherton		12 0	12 30	12-1	13
1841	CHARITY	Lord Craven		Powell		12 0	13 25	14-1	10
1842	GAY LAD	Mr. Elmore		T. Olliver		12 0	13 30	7-1	15

1843	The chase was made a HANDICAP by the late Edward William Topham, known as 'the Wizard'.								

Year	Winner	Owner	Trainer	Rider	Age	Wts. st. lbs.	Time min. sec.	S.P.	No. of Strs.
1843	VANGUARD	Lord Chesterfield		T. Olliver		11 10	—	12-1	16
1844	DISCOUNT	Mr. Quartermaine		Crickmere		10 12	—	5-1	16
1845	CUREALL	Mr. Crawford		Loft		11 5	10 47	—	15
1846	PIONEEER	Mr. Adams		Taylor	6	11 12	10 46	—	22
1847	MATTHEW	Mr. Courtney		Wynne		10 6	10 39	10-1	28
1848	CHANDLER	Capt. Little		Capt. Little		11 12	11 21	12-1	29
1849	PETER SIMPLE	Mr. Mason, Junr.		T. Cunningham		11 0	10 56	20-1	23
1850	ABD-EL-KADER	Mr. Osborne		C. Green		9 12	9 57½	—	32
1851	ABD-EL-KADER	Mr. Osborne		T. Abbot		10 4	9 59	7-1	21
1852	MISS MOWBRAY	Mr. Mason, Junr.	Dockeray	Mr. Goodman		10 4	9 58½	—	24
1853	PETER SIMPLE	Capt. Little		T. Olliver		10 10	10 37½	9-1	21
1854	BOURTON	Mr. Moseley		Tasker		11 12	9 59	4-1	20
1855	WANDERER	Mr. Sargent		J. Hanlon		9 8	10 25	25-1	20
1856	FREE TRADER	Mr. W. Barnett		G. Stevens		9 6	10 9½	25-1	21
1857	EMIGRANT	Mr. G. Hodgman		C. Boyce		9 10	10 6	10-1	28
1858	LITTLE CHARLIE	Mr. C. Capel		W. Archer		10 7	11 5	100-6	16
1859	HALF CASTE	Mr. Willoughby		C. Green	6	9 7	10 2	7-1	16
1860	ANATIS	Mr. C. Capel		Mr. Thomas		9 10	9 53	7-2	19
1861	JEALOUSY	Mr. J. Bennett		J. Kendall		9 12	10 14	5-1	24
1862	HUNTSMAN	Vicomte de Namur		H. Lamplugh		11 0	9 30	3-1	13
1863	EMBLEM	Lord Coventry		G. Stevens		10 10	11 20	4-1	16
1864	EMBLEMATIC	Lord Coventry		G. Stevens	6	10 6	11 50	10-1	25
1865	ALCIBIADE	Mr. B. J. Angell		Capt. Coventry	5	11 4	11 16	100-7	23
1866	SALAMANDER	Mr. Studd		Mr. A. Goodman	—	10 7	11 5	40-1	30
1867	CORTOLVIN	Duke of Hamilton		J. Page	—	11 13	10 42	100-6	23
1868	THE LAMB	Lord Poulett	Ben Land	Mr. Edwards	6	10 7	10 30	10-1	21
1869	THE COLONEL	Mr. M. Weyman		G. Stevens	6	10 7	10 59	13-1	22
1870	THE COLONEL	Mr. Evans		G. Stevens	7	11 12	10 9½	4-1	23
1871	THE LAMB	Lord Poulett		Mr. Thomas	—	11 4	9 36	5-1	25
1872	CASSE TETTE	Mr. E. Brayley		J. Page	—	10 0	10 14½	20-1	25
1873	DISTURBANCE	Capt. Machell	J. Richardson	Mr. J. M. Richardson	6	11 11	—	20-1	28
1874	REUGNY	Capt. Machell	J. Richardson	Mr. J. M. Richardson	6	10 12	10 4	5-1	22
1875	PATHFINDER	Mr. H. Bird		Mr. Thomas	—	10 11	10 22	100-6	19
1876	REGAL	Capt. Machell	J. Cannon	J. Cannon	5	11 3	11 14	25-1	19
1877	AUSTERLITZ	Mr. F. Hobson		Owner	5	10 8	10 10	15-1	16
1878	SHIFNAL	Mr. Nightingall		J. Jones	—	10 12	10 23	4-1	12

Year	Winner	Owner	Trainer	Rider	Age	Wts. st. lbs.	Time min. sec.	S.P.	No.of Strs.
1879	LIBERATOR	Mr. G. Moore	Moore	Mr. G. Moore	—	11 4	10 12	5-1	18
1880	EMPRESS	Mr. P. Ducrot	H. Linde	Mr. T. Beasley	5	10 7	10 20	8-1	14
1881	WOODBROOK	Capt. Kirkwood	H. Linde	Mr. T. Beasley	7	11 3	11 50	6-1	13
1882	SEAMAN	Lord Manners	Jewitt	Owner	6	11 6	10 42 3-5	10-1	12
1883	ZOEDONE	Count C. Kinsky	W. H. P. Jenkins	Owner	6	11 0	11 39	100-8	10
1884	VOLUPTUARY	Mr. H. F. Boyd	T. Wilson	Mr. E. P. Wilson	6	10 5	10 5	10-1	15
1885	ROQUEFORT	Mr. A. Cooper	Swatton	Mr. E. P. Wilson	6	11 0	10 10	100-30	19
1886	OLD JOE	Mr. A. J. Douglas	Douglas	T. Skelton	7	10 9	10 14 3-5	25-1	23
1887	GAMECOCK	Mr. E. Jay	Jordan	W. Daniels	8	11 0	10 10 1-5	20-1	16
1888	PLAYFAIR	Mr. E. W. Baird	T. Cannon	Mawson	7	10 7	10 1	40-1	20
1889	FRIGATE	Mr. M. A. Maher		Mr. T. Beasley	11	11 4	10 1 1-5	8-1	20
1890	ILEX	Mr. Masterman	Nightingall	A. Nightingall	6	10 5	10 41 4-5	4-1	16
1891	COME AWAY	Mr. W. C. Jameson	H. Beasley	Mr. H. Beasley	7	11 12	9 58	4-1	21
1892	FATHER O'FLYNN	Mr. G. C. Wilson	Wilson	Capt. E. R. Owen	7	10 5	9 48 1-5	20-1	25
1893	CLOISTER	Mr. C. G. Duff	Swatton	Dollery	9	12 7	9 32 2-5	9-2	15
1894	WHY NOT	Capt. Fenwick	Collins	A. Nightingall	13	11 13	9 45 2-5	5-1	14
1895	WILD MAN FROM BORNEO	Mr. J. Widger	Gatland	Mr. Jos Widger	7	10 11	10 32	10-1	19
1896	THE SOARER	Mr. Walker	Collins	Mr. D. G. M. Campbell	—	9 13	10 11 1-5	40-1	28
1897	MANIFESTO	Mr. H. W. Dyas	McAuliffe	T. Kavanagh	9	11 3	9 49	6-1	28
1898	DROGHEDA	Mr. G. G. M. Adamson	E. Woods	S. Gourley	6	10 12	9 43 4-5	25-1	25
1899	MANIFESTO	Mr. Bulteel	R. Collins	G. Williamson	11	12 7	9 49 4-5	5-1	19
1900	AMBUSH II	H.R.H. The Prince of Wales	A. Anthony	A. Anthony	6	11 3	10 1	4-1	16
1901	GRUDON	Mr. J. B. Bletsoe	J. Holland	A. Nightingall	11	10 0	9 47 4-5	9-1	24
1902	SHANNON LASS	Mr. A. Gorham	Hackett	D. Read	7	10 1	10 3 3-5	20-1	21
1903	DRUMCREE	Mr. H. Morrison	Sir C. Nugent	P. Woodland	9	11 3	10 9 2-5	13-2	23
1904	MOIFAA	Mr. S. Gollans	O. Hickey	A. Birch	8	10 7	9 59	25-1	26
1905	KIRKLAND	Mr. F. Bibby / Mr. L. Phillips	Thomas	F. Mason	9	11 5	9 48 1-5	6-1	25
1906	ASCETIC'S SILVER	Prince Hatzfeldt	A. Hastings	Mr. A. Hastings	9	10 9	9 34 1-5	20-1	23
1907	EREMON	Mr. S. Howard	T. Coulthwaite	Mr. A. Newey	7	10 1	9 47 1-5	8-1	23
1908	RUBIO	Major Pennant	W. Costello	H. B. Bletsoe	10	10 5	10 3 3-5	66-1	24
1909	LUTTEUR III	Mr. J. Hennessy	A. Escott	G. Parfrement	5	10 11	9 53 4-5	100-9	32
1910	JENKINSTOWN	Mr. S. Howard	T. Coulthwaite	R. Chadwick	9	10 5	10 4 4-5	100-8	25
1911	GLENSIDE	Mr. F. Bibby	Capt. Collis	Mr. J. R. Anthony	9	10 3	10 35	20-1	26
1912	JERRY M.	Sir C. Assheton-Smith	R. Gore	E. Piggott	9	12 7	10 13 2-5	4-1	24
1913	COVERTCOAT	Sir C. Assheton-Smith	R. Gore	P. Woodland	7	11 6	10 19	100-9	22
1914	SUNLOCH	Mr. T. Tyler	T. Tyler	W. J. Smith	8	9 7	9 58 4-5	100-6	20
1915	ALLY SLOPER	Lady Nelson	A. Hastings	Mr. J. R. Anthony	6	10 6	9 47 4-5	100-8	20
			1916 to 1918—**No Race**—*Owing to the War*						
1919	POETHLYN	Mrs. H. Peel	H. E. Escott	E. Piggott	9	12 7	10 8 2-5	11-4	22
1920	TROYTOWN	Major Gerrard	A. Anthony	Mr. J. R. Anthony	7	11 9	10 20 1-5	6-1	24
1921	SHAUN SPADAH	Mr. T. M. McAlpine	G. Poole	F. Rees	10	11 7	10 26	100-9	35
1922	MUSIC HALL	Mr. Hugh Kershaw	O. Anthony	L. B. Rees	9	11 8	9 55 4-5	100-9	32
1923	SERGEANT MURPHY	Mr. S. Sandford	G. Blackwell	Capt. G. H. Bennet	13	11 3	9 36	100-6	27
1924	MASTER ROBERT	Lord Airlie / Major S. Green	A. Hastings	R. Trudgill	11	10 5	9 40	25-1	31
1925	DOUBLE CHANCE	Mr. D. Gould / Mr. F. Archer	F. Archer	Major J. P. Wilson	9	10 9	9 42 3-5	100-9	33
1926	JACK HORNER	Mr. A. C. Schwartz	H. Leader	W. Watkinson	9	10 5	9 36	25-1	30
1927	SPRIG	Mrs. M. Partridge	T. R. Leader	T. Leader	10	12 4	10 20 1-5	8-1	37
1928	TIPPERARY TIM	Mr. H. S. Kenyon	J. Dodd	Mr. W. P. Dutton	10	10 0	10 23 2-5	100-1	42
1929	GREGALACH	Mrs. M. A. Gemmell	T. R. Leader	R. Everett	7	11 4	9 47 2-5	100-1	66
1930	SHAUN GOILIN	Mr. W. H. Midwood	F. Hartigan	T. Cullinan	10	11 7	9 40 3-5	100-8	41
1931	GRAKLE	Mr. C. R. Taylor	T. Coulthwaite	R. B. Lyall	9	11 7	9 32 1-5	100-6	43
1932	FORBRA	Mr. W. Parsonage	T. R. Rimell	J. Hamey	7	10 7	9 44 3-5	50-1	36
1933	KELLSBORO' JACK	Mrs. F. A. Clarke	I. Anthony	D. Williams	7	11 9	9 28	25-1	34
1934	GOLDEN MILLER	Miss Dorothy Paget	A. B. Briscoe	G. Wilson	7	12 2	9 20 2-5	8-1	30
1935	REYNOLDSTOWN	Major N. Furlong	Major N. Furlong	Mr. F. Furlong	8	11 4	9 21	22-1	27
1936	REYNOLDSTOWN	Major N. Furlong	Major N. Furlong	Mr. F. Walwyn	9	12 2	9 37	10-1	35
1937	ROYAL MAIL	Mr. H. Lloyd Thomas	I. Anthony	E. Williams	8	11 13	9 59 3-5	100-6	33

Year	Winner	Owner	Trainer	Rider	Age	Wts. st. lbs.	Time min. sec.	S.P.	No. of Strs.
1938	BATTLESHIP	Mrs. Marion Scott	R. Hobbs	B. Hobbs	11	11 6	9 29 4-5	40-1	36
1939	WORKMAN	Sir A. Maguire	J. Ruttle	T. Hyde	9	10 6	9 42 1-5	100-8	37
1940	BOGSKAR	Lord Stalbridge	Lord Stalbridge	M. A. Jones	7	10 4	9 20 3-5	25-1	30
			1941 to 1945—**No Race**—*Owing to the War*						
1946	LOVELY COTTAGE	Mr. J. Morant	T. Rayson	Capt. R. Petre	9	10 8	9 38 1-5	25-1	34
1947	CAUGHOO	Mr. J. J. McDowell	H. McDowell	E. Dempsey	8	10 0	10 3 1-5	100-1	57
1948	SHEILA'S COTTAGE	Mr. J. Procter	N. Crump	A. P. Thompson	9	10 7	9 25 2-5	50-1	43
1949	RUSSIAN HERO	Mr. W. F. Williamson	G. Owen	L. McMorrow	9	10 8	9 23 4-5	66-1	43
1950	FREEBOOTER	Mrs. L. Brotherton	R. Renton	J. Power	9	11 11	9 23 3-5	10-1	49
1951	NICKEL COIN	Mr. J. Royle	J. O'Donoghue	J. A. Bullock	9	10 1	9 47 4-5	40-1	36
1952	TEAL	Mr. H. Lane	N. Crump	A. P. Thompson	10	10 12	9 20 3-5	100-7	47
1953	EARLY MIST	Mr. J. H. Griffin	M. V. O'Brien	B. Marshall	8	11 2	9 22 4-5	20-1	31
1954	ROYAL TAN	Mr. J. H. Griffin	M. V. O'Brien	B. Marshall	10	11 7	9 32 4-5	8-1	29
1955	QUARE TIMES	Mrs. W. H. Welman	M. V. O'Brien	P. Taaffe	9	11 0	10 20 3-5	100-9	30
1956	E.S.B.	Mrs. L. Carver	T. F. Rimell	D. V. Dick	10	11 3	9 21 2-5	100-7	29
1957	SUNDEW	Mrs. G. Kohn	F. Hudson	F. T. Winter	11	11 7	9 42 3-5	20-1	35
1958	MR. WHAT	Mr. D. J. Coughlan	T. Taaffe	A. Freeman	8	10 6	9 59 4-5	18-1	31
1959	OXO	Mr. J. E. Bigg	W. Stephenson	M. Scudamore	8	10 13	9 37 1-5	8-1	34
1960	MERRYMAN II	Miss W. H. Wallace	N. Crump	G. Scott	9	10 12	9 27	13-2	26
1961	NICOLAUS SILVER	Mr. C. Vaughan	T. F. Rimell	H. Beasley	9	10 1	9 22 2-3	28-1	35
1962	KILMORE	Mr. N. Cohen	H. R. Price	F. Winter	12	10 4	9 50	28-1	32
1963	AYALA	Mr. P. B. Raymond	K. Piggott	P. Buckley	9	10 0	9 35 4-5	66-1	47
1964	TEAM SPIRIT	Mr. J. K. Goodman, Mr. Gamble North, Mr. R. B. Woodard	F. Walwyn	G. W. Robinson	12	10 3	9 47	18-1	33
1965	JAY TRUMP	Mrs. M. Stephenson	F. Winter	Mr. C. Smith	8	11 5	9 30 3-5	100-6	47
1966	ANGLO	Mr. S. Levy	F. Winter	T. Norman	8	10 0	9 52 4-5	50-1	47
1967	FOINAVON	Mr. C. P. T. Watkins	J. Kempton	J. Buckingham	9	10 0	9 49 3-5	100-1	44
1968	RED ALLIGATOR	Mr. J. Manners	D. Smith	B. Fletcher	9	10 0	9 28 4-5	100-7	45
1969	HIGHLAND WEDDING	Mr. T. H. McCoy, Junr.	G. Balding	E. P. Harty	12	10 4	9 30 4-5	100-9	30
1970	GAY TRIP	Mr. A. Chambers	T. F. Rimell	P. Taaffe	8	11 5	9 38	15-1	28
1971	SPECIFY	Mr. F. Pontin	J. Sutcliffe	J. Cook	9	10 13	9 34 1-5	28-1	38
1972	WELL TO DO	Cpt. T. A. Forster	Capt. T. A. Forster	G. Thorner	9	10 1	10 8 4-5	14-1	42
1973	RED RUM	Mr. N. H. le Mare	D. McCain	B. Fletcher	8	10 5	9 1 9-10	9-1	38
1974	RED RUM	Mr. N. H. le Mare	D. McCain	B. Fletcher	9	12 0	9 20 3-10	11-1	42
1975	L'ESCARGOT	Mr. R. Guest	D. Moore	T. Carberry	12	11 3	9 31 1-10	13-2	31
1976	RAG TRADE	Mr. P. Raymond	T. F. Rimell	J. Burke	10	10 12	9 20 9-10	14-1	32
1977	RED RUM	Mr. N. H. le Mare	D. McCain	T. Stack	12	11 8	9 30 3-10	9-1	42
1978	LUCIUS	Mrs. D. Whitaker	G. W. Richards	B. R. Davies	9	10 9	9 33 9-0	14-1	37
1979	RUBSTIC	Mr. J. Douglas	S. J. Leadbetter	M. Barnes	10	10 0	9 52 9-10	25-1	34
1980	BEN NEVIS	Mr. R. C. Stewart, Junr.	Capt. T. A. Forster	Mr. C. Fenwick	12	10 12	10 17 4-10	40-1	30
1981	ALDANITI	Mr. S. N. Embiricos	J. T. Gifford	R. Champion	11	10 13	9 47 2-10	10-1	39
1982	GRITTAR	Mr. F. Gilman	F. Gilman	Mr. C. Saunders	9	11 5	9 12 6-10	7-1	39

Index